THE TALENT SELECTION AND ONBOARDING

POCKET TOOL KIT

THE TALENT SELECTION AND ONBOARDING

POCKET TOOL KIT

How to Find, Hire, and Develop the Best of the Best

ERIKA LAMONT AND **ANNE BRUCE**

NEW YORK   CHICAGO   SAN FRANCISCO   ATHENS

LONDON   MADRID   MEXICO CITY   MILAN

NEW DELHI   SINGAPORE   SYDNEY   TORONTO

Copyright © 2014 by Erika Lamont and Anne Bruce. All rights reserved. Printed in the United States of America. Except as permitted under the United States Copyright Act of 1976, no part of this publication may be reproduced or distributed in any form or by any means, or stored in a data base or retrieval system, without prior written permission of the publisher.

1 2 3 4 5 6 7 8 9 0   DOC/DOC   1 2 0 9 8 7 6 5 4

ISBN: 978-0-07-183490-2
MHID: 0-07-183490-7

e-ISBN: 978-0-07-183491-9
e-MHID: 0-07-183491-5

Design by Mauna Eichner and Lee Fukui

Library of Congress Cataloging-in-Publication Data

Lamont, Erika.
  Talent selection and onboarding tool kit : how to find, hire, and develop the best of the best / by Erika Lamont and Anne Bruce. — 1 Edition.
    pages cm
  ISBN 978-0-07-183490-2 (alk. paper) — ISBN 0-07-183490-7 (alk. paper) 1. Employee orientation. 2. Employee motivation. 3. Employee morale. I. Bruce, Anne, 1952- II. Title.
  HF5549.5.M63L3595 2014
  658.3'1—dc23

2014013517

McGraw-Hill Education books are available at special quantity discounts to use as premiums and sales promotions, or for use in corporate training programs. To contact a representative, please visit the Contact Us page at www.mhprofessional.com.

Contents

Acknowledgments

Erika Lamont

I am grateful for the opportunity to write this, my third book, which would not have been possible without the partnership and friendship of Anne Bruce, this series' acquisition editor and my coauthor. I also appreciate the support and trust of Knox Huston, senior editor at McGraw-Hill, along with the thoughtful attention to detail from our editing team, Alice Manning, Cheryl Ringer, Scott Kurtz, Mauna Eichner, and Lee Fukui. Much of the content of this book was inspired by the conversations and relationships that I have had with several of my colleagues in talent selection and onboarding: Dave Bruce, Natalie Crede, Roy Cohen, Amy Winkler, Susan Zanon, and Rob Zedeker. I appreciate the knowledge, experience, and humor that you shared with me in our interviews. Special thanks to Todd Carter for sharing his personal onboarding story. Thank you all for your time and support!

I want to especially acknowledge the love and support of my parents, Max and Francine Buban, who have been a constant source of encouragement for every project and challenge that I have taken on in my life. Your gift of always seeing the positive in all situations keeps me going; you are really important and special to me!

My husband, Michael, and my daughters, Elizabeth and Maggie, continue to support and encourage me through every challenge, and I love and appreciate them more than they know.

Anne Bruce

It is with pleasure and great appreciation that I acknowledge the people who support my work and make a significant difference in my life and, therefore, in the lives of those who buy my books, attend my seminars and training workshops, and help keep all that I do relevant.

A very special thanks goes to my McGraw-Hill family, my esteemed publisher for 18 years. Thank you to the amazing executive editor and publisher in charge of this series, Mary Glenn, and to always-fun-to-work-with senior editor Knox Huston. I've done my best to absorb your guidance and wisdom as I've traveled the long and winding road of my publishing career. Thanks for being both colleagues and friends all these years. A special shout-out goes to our superstar editing and design team: editing liaison Scott Kurtz, Alice Manning, Cheryl Ringer, Mauna Eichner, and Lee Fukui. Thanks, Mauna, for always being available for all the late-night telephone conversations during the postproduction of this book. Your sense of humor was greatly appreciated too!

A big thank you goes to my friend and coauthor, Erika Lamont. You make integrity and intelligence look attractive in today's world. It's always a pleasure to work alongside you, and I look forward to many more collaborations. You are a wonderful collaborator who is patient, thoughtful, and generous in all that you do.

If there were a Pocket Tool Kit book titled *Awesome Friends and Family*, I'd be the author. I am truly blessed and want to say thank you here to just a few of my longtime and devoted supporters: mentor and longtime friend, literary agent, and executive editor Mark Morrow, dearest lifetime friend Kim Lehner, "sister-friend," Garrett Speakers International President, Betty Garrett, dynamic duo, best friend, and goddaughter respectively Maureen and Katie McKissick, all of the amazing and talented people at MedAmerica Billing Services, Inc. and their superstar

Educational Development Center, where we'll soon get to try out training curriculum from this book, Fired Up! AWESOME teammates Anmarie Miller, Aric Bostick, Jeni Croxford, author and novelist, DL Winter, awesome and devoted friends Keri Badach, Linda Swindling, Traci and Casey Van Attenhoven, "fascinating" leadership coach Barbara Fagan, and everyone at SourcePoint Training, team gurus and "adopted brothers" Lawrence Polsky and Antoine Gerschel, photographer Jamie Koorndyk, who shot my picture for this book, lifelong friends Harris and Carole Herman, super "Nonni" Karen Dilallo, my amazing and talented cousin and author Jeanine Finelli, my wonderful and devoted sister Rose Marie Trammell, best friends Diane Panvelle, Glenda Thomas, Phyllis Jask, who is a superstar editor and friend extraordinaire, Diana Damron, Dolly Hinshaw, and many others (too many to list here … but you know who you are). Thank you for your never-ending support and for your unconditional friendship and love.

Finally, my heartfelt appreciation and love go to my loving husband, David (20 books later you continue to sing my praises—thank you! I love you.), to my beautiful and brilliant daughter, Autumn, my amazing son-in-law Andy, my super-fun, love-of-my-life grandson, Nikolai, and to my granddaughter, whom I have yet to meet as of this writing, but you are due to arrive very soon, aka: "Baby Anniversary," I dedicate this book to you both, sweet grandson and granddaughter, and thank you for letting me be your "Grandma Fun!" It's a blast! I love my family and friends more than I can fully express within these pages. All you have done for me has allowed me to write and speak for a living and hopefully make a small but important difference in people's lives around the world. Because of you, I get to live my passion.

Introduction

"Make it simple and fast! But make it effective and get what we need." How many times have you heard this in your organization? *Simple*, *quick*, and *effective* seem to be the objectives of every business solution, especially when it comes to HR. Most managers have little time or tolerance for having to understand complex processes, go through long training classes, or read lengthy documentation. However, business and corporations are becoming increasingly complex, and so are the processes needed to support them.

So how do HR professionals or managers support a dynamic organization with demanding leadership while also being under pressure to deliver results in a way that is simple, fast, and effective? They need resources that are practical and current and that address the issues that they are facing today.

This book, *Pocket Tool Kit: Talent Selection and Onboarding*, will provide managers and HR professionals with the strategies, tips, and knowledge that they need if they are to meet these tough demands from their organizations. They will have information at their fingertips that will allow them to update their HR tool kits for successful talent selection and onboarding for years to come.

The Morphing of Talent Selection and Onboarding

Talent selection, recruiting, interviewing, and onboarding have changed so much over the last few years, and yet there are tried-and-true methods that we keep coming back to for results. The talent pools have also changed along with their expectations, so it is critical that HR professionals are able to keep up with these moving targets so that they can meet the talent needs of their organizations.

Instead of Job Hunting from Home, People Job Hunt Standing in Line at Target or Starbucks

When PepsiCo realized that 90 percent of the people who clicked through job-related e-mails from the company did so on their phones, the numbers stunned the HR department. Chris Hoyt, director of PepsiCo's global talent engagement, commented on what an eye-opener this was in an interview with *Fortune* magazine in February 2014.

In a LinkedIn survey of more than 3,000 corporate recruiters, it was evident that people were using their phones to job search, yet only 20 percent of companies were doing something about it. When PepsiCo realized the uptick in mobile visits to its career website, it built a mobile app called Possibilities to allow job seekers to look for positions, view videos on company culture, and interact with HR leaders on Twitter. The company created this mobile-friendly career site so that phone users could navigate on smaller screens more easily.[1,2]

In the past, HR executives hoped that candidates would start the process on their phones and then finish on their computers. Those days are gone. New software platforms, like iMomentous and Jibe, as well as Three Sparks, allow companies to connect their internal software systems that sort résumés and screen job hunters. LinkedIn also offers mobile services that position relevant jobs in front of job hunters who are on the go. It also helps to make the application process using a phone much easier to do.

Job Seekers Want Information in the Palm of Their Hand

Quality candidates want job information in the palm of their hand, and for companies seeking top talent, it's all about finding the best potential hires as soon as possible. It does not matter if they are at home on the couch or standing in line at Target or Starbucks. Just give them what they need to know in the palm of their hand so that it's superfast to get to and on demand. That's what hiring top talent and building a talent selection and effective onboarding tool kit is all about.

This book will deliver a way to assess your personal and professional "tool kit" and determine what needs to be added, updated, or tossed. You will also get strategies that will allow you to map your tools to different audiences, like millennials, gen Xers, and baby boomers, as well as "portfolio employees" and nontraditional workers. This book is a must-have for anyone who is involved in the hiring and developing of people—recruiters, talent management professionals, HR generalists, supervisors, managers, and aspiring leaders at all levels.

Use This Book to Make Your Place a *Great* Place to Work!

As you start reading, we'd like to offer a commonsense exercise. On the cover of this book, it says, *How to Find, Hire, and Develop the Best of the Best*. We'd like you to declare how you plan to do this. Be specific. Write it down and roll it out. We'd love to hear from you and learn the ways in which you are creating a great place to work.

Here are some of our suggestions. Aside from the tools in this book, creating a great place to work would also include a nice environment where employees can get a breath of fresh air. Maybe they can even throw a ball around or shoot hoops for 10 minutes to get the blood flowing. In elementary school, you called it recess. We think recess might be one of the things that are missing in some companies. Yeah. Everyone needs a break. Executives have been enjoying a wee bit of fun for years—golfing, racquetball club memberships, and retreats in vineyards. Maybe that's what makes them so productive and successful.

Everyone is looking for a healthier, happier work environment, whether it's at home, in an office building, on a campus, or in what is often referred to as the "third space" to work, like Starbucks, an airport lounge, or anywhere that Wi-Fi is offered.

We Hope This Pocket Tool Kit
Puts the Spring Back in Your Step

We suggest that effective talent selection and onboarding starts with turbocharged environments that will put the spring back in your step, whether you work in a cubicle, on a farm, in a glass and chrome office tower, or in a chemical plant. Our message in this introduction is to "lighten up!" Start talking kindly to people and stop yelling at them. Get rid of the stuffy consultant types and bring in the cool consultants and the work/life coaches! Reconsider mergers and acquisitions that you may have on the table and the impact they may have on your people. In other words: be nice, have fun, and bring out the best in your employees. We're here to help as your virtual coaches as you continue to use this field guide to onboard, nurture, and grow top talent.

Enjoy this go-to pocket resource and let us know how you're using it in your organization.

Your Talent Selection and Onboarding Coaches,

Erika Lamont
elamont@connectthedotsconsulting.com
and
Anne Bruce
Anne@AnneBruce.com

CHAPTER 1

The Job Market Isn't What It Used to Be
(and Neither Is the Talent)

What do you think would happen if you had to research, reapply, and interview for your current position at your current organization? Would you want the job? And would you get it? It is interesting to think about who your competition might be if you were seeking your current position and whether you would consider any other options if you found yourself in this situation. This is the situation that many of those in today's talent pool are facing and thinking about as they enter the workforce, either as new graduates, as displaced workers (companies are still downsizing to stay competitive), or as people who are currently employed but who want to make a change.

The impact of the downturn in 2008 was scary for most Americans and downright devastating for some. As we began to discuss and research the material for this book, we talked about how much things have changed in even the last four years. In early 2010, we were still talking about "the recovery" and how companies were hesitant to rehire for positions that had been eliminated as a result of the Great Recession, let alone create new jobs. Job seekers were watching anxiously for any signs in the news or from government officials that economic growth was imminent and that more good jobs were on their way. Current employees were working harder for the same or less pay and doing whatever they thought they needed to do to hang on to their jobs. Managers were being asked to do more with less, and many of them were having to become working managers, with the added expectations of delivering work products themselves as well as managing a team of people who also delivered work. Recruiters, who had braced themselves for a mass departure of baby boomers from their experienced workforce, now had far shorter open-to-hire lists, but the positions that they needed to fill were more specialized and typically required higher-level skills than were readily available in the downsized talent pool. Companies were conservative as they budgeted for the future, and adding head count was really challenging, and sometimes impossible.

This Isn't a Bad Dream—
It's Really Happening

The statistics proved that things really were as bad as they seemed. According to the U.S. Bureau of Labor Statistics website, the unemployment rates leading up to and during the recessions told the story. "In December 2007, the national unemployment rate was 5.0 percent, and it had been at or below that rate for the previous 30 months. At the end of the recession, in June 2009, it was 9.5 percent. In the months after the recession, the unemployment rate peaked at 10.0 percent (in October 2009). Before this, the most recent months with unemployment rates over 10.0 percent were September 1982 through June 1983, during which time the unemployment rate peaked at 10.8 percent."[1] Perhaps the most startling thing about this particular recession (there have actually been 10 recorded recessions between the years 1948 and 2011) was the fact that employment rates dropped faster during this one. The Bureau of Labor Statistics found that even after 47 months (just short of four years) from the official beginning point of this most recent recession, the employment rate was 4 percent *under* where it had been when the recession started.[2]

Many organizations also started to use more contract workers and consultants, many of whom were former corporate employees who now found themselves in the position of having to work as freelancers or independent consultants rather than having full-time employment. This, however, proved to be positive for some people, as they found that they enjoyed this type of project-based work and that they did not necessarily have to be an employee to do the work that they enjoyed and earn a good income. Many of these workers were women, and many of them have not yet returned to the traditional workforce. They, as well as many baby boomers (male and female), have been leading the way in increasing the number of start-up businesses in the last few years.

The Battle for Talent and Creating a Great Workplace Rages On

So that is what has set the stage and brought us to this point in what is still being called a "battle for talent," along with the desire to create a workplace that is really great. Human resources departments continue to remind us that it is hard to find the right people for certain positions and that their organizations are not filling as many positions as they were in the prerecession years. This creates double-sided pressure on both the talent selection teams and the job candidates themselves. If hiring managers have fewer positions available, they have higher expectations for the people in those positions to produce results. It seems that there is less tolerance for on-the-job training and more need for candidates who already have the necessary skills and competencies to do the job, or at least an acceptable percentage of them, before they are brought onboard. There is also a cost pressure associated with this situation, as organizations are always looking to get the "most bang for their buck" and do not necessarily want to pay more for that experience or skill level. Thus, talent recruiters must be able to balance the needs and budgets of their organizations with the current candidate pool.

The Bureau of Labor Statistics has some projections for the next nine years. It predicts continued shrinking of the U.S. labor force, leading to less economic growth overall. This is a function of baby boomers retiring and there being fewer workers in the following generations to replace them. However, as always, there are bright spots, and those are projected growth in most sectors of the economy, especially healthcare, social assistance, certain service-providing industries, and construction. The decline in manufacturing, agriculture, information, and utilities will continue. Almost one-third of the growth will occur in the healthcare and social assistance categories. This information is important from several perspectives.

1. In the industries that will experience growth, talent recruiters must understand that they may need to be creative when looking to replace or add workers.

2. For the declining industries, talent recruiters may be able to hire "more for less" as the numbers of desirable positions shrink.

It will continue to prove challenging for HR professionals to match talent to open positions appropriately. The "fit" is what is important, and the criteria for that fit are changing as fast as the demographics are changing.

Speed Dating for Talent

How do you know whether the people who are in your candidate pool are right for your organization? The selection and interviewing process can feel a bit like speed dating to find the "right" person for the job. As in speed dating, impressions are made early and are sometimes based on information that may or may not be an indicator of success. For example, research shows that speed daters make a decision about a person in the first 3 to 30 seconds based on factors like height and age rather than on any previous marriages, religion, or smoking habits.[3]

So, the challenge of matching talent and organizations is as complex as couples' matchmaking, and as in matchmaking, unfortunately, relationship decisions are often based on factors that seem like less-than-scientific predictors of success.

Here is a quick-start way to determine whether you are attracting the people you want. First, what type of employment brand does your organization have? It is critical that you discuss and shape a message about how you want to be viewed by potential candidates in the marketplace and also how you differentiate yourself from your competition. Formal outlets for promoting your employment brand, like your website, your recruiting materials, and your social media messages, are important; however, just as critical, and maybe more so, is how your selection team and your hiring managers represent your brand. Are your recruiting tools and interview questions consistent with your brand? Are you gathering data from your candidates to know if you are on track? Are you representing the true culture of your organization, or is the "sales pitch" culture a lot different from the real one? People are more savvy than ever when it comes to determining the authenticity of how an organization represents itself. Information on how an organization's employees really feel about it is readily available to validate or disprove a recruiter's assertions.

So where can an organization find the type of talent it needs to achieve its goals? Our recruiting friends know many tricks of the trade to uncover both active and passive job seekers, and there are both advantages and trade-offs with both of these pools of talent.

Many recruiters are finding that passive job seekers are the most desirable and provide them with the best networking opportunities.

> Quick definition: *passive candidates* are those people who are gainfully employed and are relatively happy in their current roles but who may consider changing jobs.

Both active and passive job candidates must also be able to self-select your organization, but if they are to do so, you need to ensure that they can do it easily through your company website and your employment website. There is an increasing expectation that information about companies and their job opportunities is available 24/7 and from any type of mobile device.

Let's go back to the first question of this chapter: If you had to research, apply, and interview for your current job and your current organization, would you? Or could you?

Test Your Wow Factor

Table 1.1 gives you a quick way to gauge your organization's *approachability factor* from a job seeker's perspective (just as with a quiz in one of those magazines, you can test your organization's wow factor for potential candidates!).

Table 1.1 **What Do Job Candidates Experience from Your Employment Website?** Ratings: 4 = Yes, nailed it!; 3 = Sort of, meets our needs; 2 = Not really, needs work; 1 = No, big opportunity	
Question	**Rating**
1. Is your website visually attractive, up-to-date, and interesting?	
2. Is you website easy to navigate and intuitive?	
3. Do job candidates understand who you are, what you do, and what you value?	
4. Are the open positions easy to find, well organized, and well defined?	
5. Is there information about what it's actually like to work here?	
6. Can job candidates interact with you to ask questions and provide feedback?	
7. Do job candidates interact with you the way you want them to?	
8. Are there strategic touch points of communication with candidates?	
9. Are candidates interacting with you the way you intended?	
10. Is the feedback from candidates what you want it to be?	
Total	

Scoring Results

32–40 = You have the foundation to allow job candidates to opt in to your organization, and it's likely that they will be the candidates you seek.

31–25 = You are probably doing fairly well, but you may be missing some top candidates.

24–18 = You have some real opportunities to improve your approachability; pick one or two areas in which to improve.

18 or less = You should take a step back and reevaluate how you want to represent yourself as an employer. Start with defining your employment brand and work from there.

TIPS AND TAKEAWAYS FROM THIS CHAPTER

- Good (and great) talent is still hard to find.

- The job market is not rebounding to prerecession levels.

- Talent has responded by entering the contract and consultant workforce or starting businesses.

- Organizations must position themselves to be approachable to job candidates.

CHAPTER 2

HR in the New Landscape: Lean, Flat, and Stretched to the Max

Job seekers were not the only ones affected by the "adjustment" in the economy caused by the Great Recession. HR professionals in every industry and every size organization were affected as well. Because Human Resources is still an overhead expense for companies, it is always a target for cost reduction when things get tight. For this reason, many HR leaders were getting creative in finding ways to save money from their budgets—reorganizations, loss of new positions, or head-count reductions—in those areas where the big money is spent.

Work Strategically, Not Harder

Many organizations did the "make or buy" analysis and decided to outsource noncore activities or functions and pay other providers to carry them out—the HR BPO, or human resources business process outsourcing. Payroll and benefits administration, recruitment, performance management, and training were all functions that it was popular to identify as having the potential to be outsourced and save costs. When they were outsourced, in many cases the results were mixed. HR generalists were supposed to have had these administrative tasks removed from their plates so that they could focus on the needs of their internal clients at a more strategic level. What typically occurred was less than strategic. The HR business partners (HRBPs) often had to fill the gaps that were left when internal experts were replaced by external providers. A great deal of organizational knowledge left the building with those employees, and the external providers weren't able to make it up. As a result, the HR business partners were now saddled with the need to address issues and put out fires created by this lack of cultural and organizational knowledge. In some organizations, service from HR got worse, resulting in distrust from the rest of the organization. Because of this distrust, HR was viewed as an incompetent partner and was excluded from key conversations and meetings in which it should have been an influential and strategic participant. This left organizational leaders as the ones who had to think more about talent as a strategy for business results; some did this well, but others struggled. Operational and line leaders often find it difficult to step back from the work and think about what talent they have, what talent they need, and how to position their functions to get that talent and achieve the objectives that the organization expects of them.

What's HR Got to Do with It?

Every HR professional we know or with whom we come in contact tells us that if you don't do the basics right, you don't get invited to do the good stuff. The long-standing complaint of human resources professionals is that their senior leaders viewed them as transactional administrators, not key business partners. However, the paradox of this problem is one that is widely known. If you master the basics, like payroll, benefits, employee relations, hiring, and firing, you are able to sell yourself as so much more.

The human resources business partner role was first introduced by David Ulrich in his 1997 book *Human*

Resource Champions.[1] His original definition is illustrated in Figure 2.1.

Figure 2.1   **Human Resources Business Partner Roles**

The order of the components is deliberate and reflected at the time what the priority that Ulrich believes the business partner should give to each one; first, to be seen as that strategic partner, than have the technical expertise in human resources administration. Executing on the basics is often the price of admission for the strategy. Next then the leader must be an employee champion as well as "chief change agent" for the organization.

The emphasis on "business" in the business partner role is critical. No one else in the organization typically cares about the latest employment regulations or compensation strategy unless it directly affects him or her. So, HRBPs must first apply everything they do to the context of the business, by the business, and for the business. It must pass the "why does the business care about this?" test before they introduce it to their client groups.

Ulrich has since updated his definition of the HR business partner in his study of HR competencies in 2012.

His new definition looks a lot like Figure 2.2 with a few key wording changes.

Figure 2.2 **2012 Human Resources Business Partner Roles**

Here is how he defines each role:

- The *strategic positioner* has the ability to translate business knowledge into organizational action.

- The *credible activist* builds relationships of trust and influence.

- The *capability builder* is able to discern the organizational culture and mold it to its desired state.

- The *change champion* can initiate and sustain organizational change.

- The *HR innovator* can integrate best practices, new technology, and new ideas into sound HR practices that drive the organization forward. Human Resources is being asked to step up to a role that will inevitably be a critical component of the success (or lack of it) of an organization.

Getting Out of the Kitchen and to the Table

In our work with client organizations, we find that there are human resources managers who truly believe that they are working at the level of HR business partner yet are surprised when their internal clients are not engaged in their conversations or are constantly canceling meetings with them. These HR professionals have great intentions and are performing what they think is business-critical work; however, they are not perceived as doing so by their functional peers or by senior leaders. Shifting the mindset concerning what the role of Human Resources means to the business is critical in bridging this gap. The HR manager must first think about the business needs, then be able to talk about how Human Resources can support those needs. If the conversation focuses on anything other than how HR supports, enhances, and adds critical value to a business process or solves a key business problem, then the HR manager loses another opportunity to "be at the table." Too often, HR is still "in the kitchen" by being more concerned with the latest update of the PeopleSoft systems, a new applicant tracking system, the updates to the executive compensation plan, or the reworking of the performance management process. Although most of the business leaders would not label these initiatives as necessarily irrelevant for the business, they would not be likely to see them as projects that needed much of their personal time or attention. These leaders would put those items in the "HR bucket" and not really see them as core business activities. HR professionals who are primarily focused on these topics will lose the opportunity to engage with leaders in a consultative and business-relevant way.

Being a more consultative partner requires some careful thought about and preparation for the interactions that an HR manager has with both individual leaders and the larger leadership team. The "quick quiz" given here will help you start to think about how you are positioning yourself in the organization.

QUICK QUIZ

Are You an HR Business Partner or an HR Process Partner?

Answer these five questions to see if you are functioning as a true business partner or if you are more focused on HR process work.

(continues)

1. Do you regularly attend your client groups' staff meetings, strategy discussions, and brainstorming meetings?

2. Do you regularly touch base with the leaders of your client groups?

3. Do these leaders ask for your advice?

4. Are you asked to share or present your ideas about how the departments you support meet their business objectives?

5. Is your calendar full of more client group meetings than HR meetings?

A "yes" to all five of these questions indicates that you are most likely working as an HR business partner. A no answer to three or more may suggest that you have the opportunity to modify your role.

What's in a Name?

Not only are the roles of human resources professionals changing, but, as the title of this chapter suggests, the structure and makeup of the departments are not what they used to be either. HR enjoyed a bit of a reinvention in the late 1980s and early 1990s when most organizations changed from personnel departments to human resources departments. One executive recruiter whom Erika interviewed for this book recalls the conversation that he had with his boss at the time, who said to him, "We are Personnel now, but very soon we'll be Human Resources. Just go with it." The intention of the upgrade in naming this function was to draw attention to the value that high-quality talent brings to an organization and the fact that an organization's employees, not its accounts receivables, cash, real estate, or equipment, are its real assets. The trend now is to upgrade the name again, and some, especially larger companies, are calling it People Department and Human Capital, with Talent Management typically being as a subset of this larger classification. Talent Management usually includes all recruiting, onboarding, development (individual, management, and leadership), and sometimes succession planning. However, as companies were downsizing during the recession, Human Resources has been squeezed and is often left with a skeleton crew to pilot the talent ship.

The most successful HR professionals have been able to understand that these changes were inevitable and figured out a way to work with them. They focused on knowing their business and forging relationships that would add value. This applies for both the business partners who support the day-to-day needs of the organization and those on the talent management team.

Table 2.1, "HR Business Knowledge Worksheet," is a tool to help you improve your business knowledge.

Table 2.1 **HR Business Knowledge Worksheet** This resource will help you jump-start your business knowledge or deepen what you already know. With this increased business acumen, you can position yourself as a real partner, not just an administrator of processes and procedures.		
What HR Should Know	**Where to Find It**	**Your Answers Here**
What is your business model? How does your organization make money?		
Who are your customers?		
Who are your competitors?		
What is your current business strategy? How is it different from your competitors'?		
What new markets, technology, or products is your company considering?		
What is the timing for these?		

What HR Should Know	Where to Find It	Your Answers Here
How will these new strategies affect the talent that is needed?		
Are there any particular obstacles that your organization is facing now?		

Putting Your New Head Set to Work

Preparation, study, and reading will all help you build your competencies as an HR business partner; however, there is no better teacher than actual experience. By putting yourself into situations where you will be called upon to offer an idea, a perspective, or a solution, you position yourself to gain such experience. Attend as many operational meetings as possible and constantly think about how your overall talent strategy and its processes either support or restrict business objectives. Consider the questions that the business leaders ask and the problems that they face. How can talent selection, onboarding, or development affect these issues? Create scenarios so that when you are asked, you can offer a thoughtful perspective.

You may feel impatient when the organization and its leaders do not immediately recognize your efforts and your newly formed skills; however, it is important to understand that time is required for this recognition to fully develop and for your "HR brand" to change. Younger HR managers are especially vulnerable to this frustration, thinking that after a few successful projects and good conversations with senior leaders, they are ready to be seen as an equal partner and, in fact, be promoted! Persistence, patience, and a good mentor are the key ingredients that you need in order to fully develop as a true HR business partner in any organization.

Line Leaders Have a Role

The line leaders also have some skin in the game as it relates to engaging with HR as a business partner. As executive coaches, we often talk with our clients about how "we teach or train people how to treat us" with our behaviors and interactions with them. This is powerful stuff! Line leaders can train or teach their HR partners to be more strategic advisors by asking for their opinions not only on HR matters but also on operational issues. HR partners should not feel intimidated by or unqualified to respond to these types of requests, because in almost every situation there is a "human factor" associated with them. And this should encourage the HR partner to continue to learn more about the business and what its leaders are struggling with. It is probably obvious, yet worth mentioning, that in these situations, the HR partner must respond appropriately and quickly in order to gain credibility and trust with these leaders. There won't be a lot of tolerance for "I'll get back to you on that" or "I'll need a couple of weeks to put that together" responses before the line leaders move on. The flip side to this is that managers shouldn't let HR professionals off the hook, but should continue to put pressure on them to learn the business and come to the table with proposals to support it. In turn, HR partners can also train and teach their line leaders to include them in these discussions by making time for department staff meetings, weighing in on "non-HR" topics, and presenting talent-based solutions to business problems.

TIPS AND TAKEAWAYS FROM THIS CHAPTER

- Organizations have changed, and so has Human Resources.

- Consider how your organization and the way it "uses" HR have changed.

(continues)

- Identify what your company really needs if it is to meet its goals.

- Assess your HR partners against the new definition of an HR business partner.

- Grow your business knowledge to be a better partner.

- Managers should expect HR to fill the business partner role and spell out what they need from it.

CHAPTER 3

Where Is the Talent and What Is It Thinking?

Many organizations, possibly even yours, may be asking this very question because they have not been successful in finding, recruiting, or hiring the talent that they need if they are to hit their business targets. Some blame the talent pool and complain that the good talent is already taken and that the current job seekers are not up to par. When asked to assess the current talent pool, Roy Cohen, vice president and chief human resource officer at TruGreen, answers, "It depends on two things: the strength of your brand and the market. The talent is out there, but we have found that your location, especially after the collapse of the housing market, really makes a difference to top candidates. They don't want to move."

Accommodations Needed

Cohen's experience is similar to that of many HR executives who are trying to recruit the next generation of company leaders. He says that there are always two factors that affect a candidate's willingness to relocate for a job. One is the value of the candidate's current home (is he or she underwater on its value?), and the second is the level of trust the candidate has in the organization—will this company exist in five years? Because TruGreen is located in Memphis, Tennessee, Cohen knows all too well the challenges of getting people, especially top talent for leadership roles, to relocate. "You need to be accommodating," Cohen advises. "For example, giving people more transition time to relocate and allowing them time for a child to graduate or for a spouse to find a job in the new city can really make a difference. You open up your options as an employer if you don't insist on being 'eyeball to eyeball' with people until you really need to be." This idea of working virtually, even temporarily, can have a significant positive impact in terms of expanding your talent pool. As each employee's situation is unique, the typical time frame for most companies is to allow up to 12 months for such a transition. Organzations need to be accommodating, but also fiscally responsible.

Take the quick quiz in Table 3.1 to determine whether your organization is accommodating today's changing talent pool.

Table 3.1 **Are You Accommodating Today's Talent?**	
Question	**Yes/No**
1. Have you ever delayed a start date to accommodate a new hire?	
2. Do you regularly review your relocation policy and update it?	
3. Do you allow for exceptions to the relocation policy based on a particular situation?	
4. Do you have resources available to make these exceptions?	
5. Does the organization have precedents for employees or leaders working remotely?	
6. Do you have technology that would support working remotely?	
7. Have you determined which jobs need to be on-site and which ones could be remote?	
8. Are you getting regular feedback from candidates?	
9. Are you integrating this feedback into your policies and practices?	
10. Are you measuring trending feedback to make decisions about your talent strategy?	
Number of yes responses	**/10**
Number of no responses	**/10**

People Want to Know Your Story

Connecting with the right candidates for your organization is a lot like dating. You check each other out: Do you like and value the same things? Is there a connection that could be leveraged for a long-term deeper and more productive relationship for both of you? Because of the increasing transparency and availability of information about companies, it is best if you create your employment brand strategy and describe it by telling a story. Potential candidates want to know who you are as an organization, what you stand for, how you reward people, and what the future looks like. Talent professionals know the danger of "holding workers hostage" with salary or other incentives when they really don't have a passion for the organization. When you truthfully describe your company's culture, candidates can opt in or out, depending on their personal circumstances.

Here are some points to consider when you are trying to create or improve your employment brand.

YOUR EMPLOYMENT BRAND MUST:

- Be easy to describe in a few sentences.

- Reflect your vision, mission, and values.

- Represent your culture.

- Match and complement your consumer brand.

- Be validated by leaders, tenured employees, and new hires.

- Be promoted both internally and externally.

- Stay fresh and updated.

What Makes Your Employment Brand Relevant? World-Class Organizations Set the Bar High

Whole Foods Market. Transparency is part of its brand. Every employee can see everyone else's salary. Employees also vote on new hires.

Nordstrom. Known for its "no rule book" philosophy, the upscale retailer continues its mantra: "Our one rule is to always use good judgment."

Starbucks. This firm is still offering benefits and stock to employees working 20 hours a week and is known for offering lots of opportunities to work up the ladder.

Mars. The candy maker's pet food division (Pedigree and Whiskas) allows employees to bring their pets to work.

(continues)

> *St. Jude Children's Research Hospital.*   Where fun saves lives. The noted hospital celebrates success with hula hoops, Silly String wars, and musical chairs.
>
> *American Express.*   What brands this financial giant? One thing is diversity and lots of employee networks that celebrate religious affiliations and many other characteristics.

No Commitment, No Problem

Another thing that manager or talent selection professionals have learned is that people are not necessarily looking for careers anymore; they are seeking opportunities. These opportunities may take the form of traditional jobs, temporary assignments, or contracted projects. The duration of each of these opportunities varies as much as the types of assignments. Recruiters are discovering that the members of today's talent pool are making decisions about their lifestyles first, then making choices about how to support those lifestyles. This is especially true for the more recent generations who have entered the workforce, generation X and the millennials (generation Y). They, even more than their baby boomer predecessors, have determined their priorities and are matching their work lives to those priorities. See the sidebar for a description of each generation.

There has never before been a workforce that has had representation from four generations. Here are how these generations are widely defined:

- *Traditionalists* Born after World War I, they have a strong work ethic, are loyal, and have respect for hierarchy.

- *Baby boomers.* Born between 1945 and 1960, they are competitive and hardworking, and they want consensus-based decisions.

- *Generation X.* Born between 1961 and 1981, they value relationships and want a clear career path, a collaborative work environment, and work/life balance.

- *Millennials or generation Y.* Born between 1982 and 1997, they want the opportunity to build skills for the future, customizable rewards for work, and the ability to blend personal and work life with strong values.

(continues)

> Now more than ever, there are employees from all different age groups working together, and this creates a new dynamic. Organizations that understand and manage this dynamic can turn it into a competitive advantage and get the best out of all their people.

It is important for talent management teams that they help their organizations understand the changing preferences of the current talent pool. By providing them with the most recent information about these trends, the talent management team can allow managers to look at their talent needs differently and perhaps a little more creatively in order to open up more sources of potential candidates. Seasonal, part-time, or contract roles offer opportunities for different segments of the work pool. On the flip side, combining roles may offer a better, more interesting job for a higher-skilled worker and create a more efficient, lower-cost solution for the organization. Managers who are willing to be innovative and flexible will be more successful in this changing talent landscape.

Expectations Are Changing

With the warp speed at which change is taking place in our world, it is no surprise that the expectations of the current talent pool are changing too. Many of these differing expectations result from the generational differences in the talent pool. As we mentioned, now is the time when the greatest number of generations is represented in the workplace. Let's take a deeper dive into what each of these groups values and expects from its employers.

Traditionalists

Although there are fairly few traditionalists left in the workplace, there still are a few, and they are most likely to be people who founded or own a company or who are leaders in a family-owned one. Traditionalists not only are comfortable with hierarchy, they really don't know any other way to organize things. They lived through the Great Depression, and they tend to be conservative with their money and their lifestyles. Newer technology is pretty foreign to them, yet they understand its importance. They value loyalty and longevity in an employer-employee relationship. Here are some of the qualities that employers must be aware of in order to manage this group successfully.

TRADITIONALISTS TEND TO:

- Be extremely loyal.

- Respect authority, to the point of submission.

- Be tech-challenged.

- Have a strong work ethic.

Baby Boomers

This group represents the largest population among the different generational groups; hence the word *boomer* in the name. The single most significant historical event for this group is the U.S. landing on the moon, so they tend to be proud, patriotic, and competitive. How these qualities translate for employers is that boomers want to be recognized for putting in long hours and working hard. They value consensus-based decision making and continued opportunities to learn. Here are some of the qualities that employers must be aware of in order to manage this group successfully.

BABY BOOMERS TEND TO:

- Embrace corporate structure.

- Be comfortable with formality.

- Want to be in charge.

- Love to win, as they are competitive.

- Make more statements and ask fewer questions.

Generation X

Of the three most dominants generations in today's talent pool (Baby Boomers, Generation X and the Millennials) this is the smallest. Generation X was very much affected by the downsizing of corporate America, as well as the loss of trust created by the Enron scandal and the emotional loss caused by the *Challenger* disaster in 1986. Because of these events, this generation tends to be less trustful of organizations and more concerned about acquiring the skills and experiences that will build their career portfolios so that they do not "put all their eggs" in one corporate basket. Additionally, they feel squeezed between the boomers, who aren't retiring (these are most of today's current leaders), and the millennials, who are cheaper to hire and seem to have a built-in kinship with the boomers. Here are some of the qualities that employers must be aware of in order to manage this group successfully.

GENERATION XERS TEND TO:

- Value having options.

- Mistrust the corporate structure.

- Have strong relationship skills.

- Embrace technology, diversity, and change.

- Be seen as "not as engaged at work" because of personal commitments.

Generation X has also very different expectations of its employers. Here is what generation Xers want in an organization:

1. The ability and opportunity to leverage their relationships

2. Strong teamwork and a collaborative environment

3. A diverse leadership team (in terms of gender, ethnicity, and views)

4. Clear career paths

5. A balance between work and personal lives

Millennials or Generation Y

The millennials are the second-largest group in the workforce today, next to the boomers. Generation Y has grown up with technology integrated into almost every part of life. People in this group were raised on praise, with every effort being rewarded. Not only are they accustomed to praise, but they are self-confident and speak their minds freely. They were also mostly raised in two-income families, with high divorce rates, so they tend to be independent.

The single most significant event for millennials was 9/11. They saw how fragile life can be, and this has driven them to be family-centric and to demand more balance and flexibility in their work lives. Although they share this last quality of demand for life balance with generation X, they tend to take it to a whole new level.

Here are the things that those in Generation Y look for in an employer and that should be considered by organizations that want to attract them:

1. The opportunity to develop skills for the future

2. The chance to display their strong values

3. Customizable reward and recognition

4. Blended work and personal lives

5. Clear career paths—the same as generation X

How Am I Doing?
The Importance of Feedback

There is a bit of a running joke among managers and HR professionals that the "younger generations" (mostly generation Y, and now even younger) is constantly asking for feedback. The funny part is, they ask so often that hardly anything has had the opportunity to change before they ask again. Sometimes, the only feedback that a manager can give a millennial is to quit asking for so much feedback! However, this situation brings to light yet another difference in the expectations of each generational group in the workplace. Boomers tend to go on the "no news is good news" standard until they have their annual performance reviews. Any feedback between these reviews is viewed as "extra," welcomed if it is positive and often feared and disliked if it is constructive or viewed as being negative. However, baby boomers appreciate straightforward and timely feedback.

By contrast, generation Xers are very much concerned about building relationships before any kind of feedback is given or received. The credibility of the sender of the message is extremely important to this group. Additionally, this group wants and expects a variety of options for giving, receiving. and acting on feedback. Thus, 360-degree tools, feedback focus groups, exit interviews, and other such methods have been created to accommodate this type of need.

Lastly, the millennials have what seems to be an unquenchable thirst for feedback in both their professional relationships and their personal ones. Some of this can be blamed on the constant contact created by mobile phones and social media and the ability to "like" and "comment" on almost everything imaginable. Organizations must understand this new reality and adapt their feedback mechanisms to provide both frequent and two-way feedback channels. Companies also need to manage this group's expectations appropriately so that these people have a more realistic picture of what type of feedback they will get and when they will get it. A "no news is good news" approach will frustrate people in this group and is most likely to drive them to find a more feedback-friendly organization.

TIPS AND TAKEAWAYS FROM THIS CHAPTER

- Be accommodating to today's talent pool.

- Understand the dynamics of each generation in the workplace.

- Adapt your practices to match the expectations of each group.

- Decide which generation will do best at meeting your business objectives.

(continues)

- Create your organizational brand and stand by your company culture.

- Learn the values of prospective employees regarding work and life balance.

- Match your talent strategy to the needs of each generational group.

CHAPTER 4

The Talent Selection Tool Kit: Tried-and-True and What's New

A friend and client colleague, Susan Zanon, calls herself "old-fashioned." If you met her, you would not necessarily use those words to describe her. She is the director of talent acquisition for Lane Bryant; sits in a modern office building surrounded by the latest colors, styles, and fashion trends; and can ping, post, tweet, and friend with the best of them!

> Lane Bryant is a specialty retailer, operating more than 800 stores nationwide, with a mission to empower every woman to feel confident and beautiful, regardless of her size. In 2012, Ascena Retail Group, Inc., acquired Lane
>
> *(continues)*

Bryant, making it part of a leading national specialty retailer with five distinct brands. With more than 3,800 stores throughout the United States and Canada, Ascena realizes revenues of more than $4.5 billion.

She looks and speaks like someone who is firmly based in the current trends and whims of a specialty retail environment. However, when you listen to Susan describe her more than 20-year career in talent selection and onboarding, you will hear the words "old-fashioned." She is referring to the tried-and-true methods that she has relied on for getting the best talent matchups for every organization she has worked for. She explains that is no substitute for relationship building and networking in order to find the right people for those open positions.

Always Interviewing

When asked to explain this a bit more, Susan says that she is "basically always interviewing," and that can be interpreted as using every conversation and interaction as an opportunity to get to know someone better and understand his or her experiences, skills, and passions, as well as figuring out whom he or she knows. A sharp recruiter can hit the payload of information that will allow her to fill a current opening or give her some key contact that will result in a hire several weeks, months, or years down the road. Susan advises recruiters not to "wait until your company is in panic mode" as it tries to fill positions, but to "keep the pipeline full and active" with people who could potentially fit the bill. Even if the people you talk to are not interested in changing jobs at that time, it is possible, and even probable, that at some time in the future their circumstances will change and a passive candidate will become an active one.

There are a few tips and tricks that seasoned recruiters use to keep their pipelines full and leverage their networks and relationships to do so. Meeting and talking with people is the most obvious and the most effective. Leveraging social media is a way that recruiters have blended the new tools with the tried-and-true ones.

Here are a few good conversation starters and networking questions from the pros that you can use to keep your pipeline active. Use these for both in-person conversations and electronic ones.

- We need to catch up! What's going on in your company?

(continues)

- Tell me what you are working on now. Do you enjoy it? Why or why not?

- Do you enjoy what you are doing right now?

- Do you see yourself doing this for a while?

- If you could do anything, what would it be?

- What's your dream job/organization/lifestyle?

- Have you ever considered doing _____?

- Do you know someone in your network who might be interested in ___?

- Can you introduce me to someone (by e-mail, LinkedIn, Facebook, or Twitter) who may be considering _____?

- I have a great article about _____ that I will send you, and we can stay in touch.

- Let's stay in touch—what way do you prefer (e-mail, phone, social media)?

Get Paid to Talk to People

With so much attention being given to the baby boomers and their "second acts," don't miss the opportunity to take an inventory of where people are, what experiences they've had, and how these may match the needs of your organization. Boomers typically have created large personal networks, and now they have expanded those networks through their children (the current generation X or millennials) and their friends' children. This is a great way to tap into a double network and find the skill sets and experiences you are looking for in your candidates.

Because good communication is a no-brainer for recruiting the best talent, HR professionals have had to adapt some of their behaviors because of the explosion of the use of technology, especially social media. My recruiting friends tell me that in many ways, social media is both a blessing and a curse. Amy Winkler, recruiter at Smith's Medical, explains that the use of technology in recruiting really depends on the part of the country you are in. She has found that candidates and companies on the West Coast are much more comfortable with using Facebook, for example, to find jobs and job applicants than, say, those in the Midwest or on the East Coast. Although most people do use LinkedIn, she explains, the farther east you go, the somewhat more traditional the methods of communication become. The exception to this is the use of text messages. "Texting a candidate," she says, "is really not OK in the Midwest, but it is totally fine on both the East and the West coasts."

One of Amy's most tried-and-true recruiting methods, and also one that most recruiters rely on, is referral.
She explains that there is no replacement for a good referral because you know and trust the person from whom you
have received it, and for her, referrals have always proved to
be successful. This is not to suggest that you don't still put
these candidates through your typical screening process,
but it is certainly more likely that they will get through the
first few steps quickly because the referral has done some
of that screening for you already.

The questions used for getting referrals are largely dependent on your relationship with the person you are talking
with, but here are some suggestions that work in various
situations:

- Sounds like you are pretty satisfied where you are.
  Is there anyone you know who might be interested in another opportunity?

- You are really connected in your field; can you
  think of anyone that I might talk with about this
  position?

- It's been great talking with you and learning
  what's going on in your organization. Do you

> know of someone with a similar position that I
> might talk with?
>
> • What professional groups (publications, blogs,
>   websites, conferences, and so on) do you use to
>   stay up on the trends in your field?

Note: Do you know any other recruiters? Don't forget to tap into them for names and leads, and be prepared to share some of yours, too.

Résumés Required

All the recruiters we interviewed debunked the idea that companies do not really use or rely on résumés anymore—they are not as important as they used to be. Although the paper résumé has gone the way of the dinosaurs, companies still require and use résumés to make the first decisions about candidates. Talent management systems and applications are used to store, prequalify, and organize electronic résumés so that companies can pull the information out when it is needed. However, recruiters are still asking for and reviewing individual résumés to find and qualify candidates. This proves that there is still a human factor in selecting candidates to interview.

The use of key words on résumés is one of the ways in which talent management systems companies sell their software. The applications scan the résumés for predetermined keywords that the organization has defined for the position it is filling. According to one seasoned recruiter, the use and importance of keywords is "blown out of proportion, because we do actually look at the résumés that come through." Other recruiters agree and complain that the whole process can get too impersonal if companies rely only on their talent management systems and their keyword searches.

According to a December 11, 2013, article by LinkedIn contributor Victor Luckerson, these are the 10 worst buzzwords to use on a résumé:

- Responsible

- Strategic

- Creative

- Effective

- Patient

- Expert

- Organizational

- Driven

- Innovative

- Analytical

Innovative is by far the worst offender, according to the LinkedIn study, because it has made the list four years in a row.[1]

Hit Your Target

The more specific you can be about the qualifications for your open jobs, the better. There are now dozens of career boards that are dedicated to an industry or job type. Dice.com, for example, targets information technology professionals, Idealist.org lists nonprofit jobs, eFinancial Careers.com is the source for financial careers, Mediabistro .com sources media jobs, and HEALTHeCAREERS.com matches candidates with positions in the medical field.

Staying up on the job boards in your industry and knowing how to navigate the universal ones is an important tool in the talent selection kit, as these web resources are becoming more nichelike and specialized to attract their preferred audiences; however, most experienced talent management professionals and hiring managers will say that they do not rely exclusively on these websites but use them as an additional source for names and résumés of potential candidates.

The most popular universal job boards include:

- CareerBuilder

- Cool Works

- Indeed

- LinkedIn

- LinkUp

- Monster

- Simply Hired

- US.jobs

Are You the Right Fit for Some of These Stellar Organizations?

- *Umpqua Bank.* This Portland bank is into motivation. Employees gather every morning for what the company calls a "motivation moment." Only motivated employees need apply!

- **Navy Federal Credit Union.** If you're into families first, this is the credit union for you. The world's largest credit union provides on-site childcare.

- **Zappos.com.** The most successful online shoe retailer wants you to enjoy living in Las Vegas. It is spending hundreds of millions of dollars to develop the entire neighborhood where it has relocated so that employees can enrich their careers and their social lives.

Best Behavior

The one consistent theme that people who are involved in any type of talent selection talk about is finding the right fit for their open jobs. One senior talent management leader, Natalie Crede from Safelite AutoGlass, describes the evolution of matching candidates to positions as moving from more transactional to a focus on skills and experiences, and now to a focus on behaviors and fit. Natalie and her senior leader peers often say, "You can't teach nice!" Safelite is undergoing its second transformation to being completely "people powered and customer driven," so it needs to have employees with the right attitudes and behaviors. The secret to finding these types of people is through behavioral interviewing. This type of interviewing probably is not anything radically new, but it has become more popular over the last several years, and most organizations have adopted it in some form.

Safelite is doing some pretty progressive stuff by investing its time and resources in using assessment centers that employ role playing. Role playing gives interviewers the best environment for testing how potential employees respond to certain situations. Answers to interview questions can be "rehearsed and artificial," according to Crede, but by asking candidates to respond to real scenarios from case studies based on actual business interactions, Safelite gets much better information about how people react in stressful or challenging situations. The results speak for themselves, and there has been a marked improvement in the type of talent that the company is attracting and hiring. The leaders are now seeing that this method of selection works, and they are realizing the benefits through business results. The first group to notice the increased talent levels was the regional trainers, who said that they saw a marked improvement in the caliber of people going through the training that is required of employees upon joining the organization.

Tables 4.1 and 4.2 are a sample interview guide and evaluation form for an individual contributor role that can be used to introduce or enhance your behavioral interviewing process.

Table 4.1 **Sample Interview Guide—Individual Contributor**	
Candidate:	
Interviewer:	
Date:	

Question	Response
1. Please tell me how you define the role of (insert title here).	
2. Tell me about how you approach your work. Please give me an example of how this style has enabled you to be successful. Please tell me about a time when your style has not been effective.	
3. Please give me an example of a difficult issue or problem that you had to solve. What was the outcome?	
4. Tell me about your process for setting goals and holding yourself to them.	*(continues)*

Question *(continued)*	Response
5. What are your career goals? Where are you now relative to those goals, and what specifically are you doing to achieve them?	
6. How do you define the customers of this role or function?	
7. Please share both a positive and a negative customer interaction that you have had recently.	
8. (Add a specific job-related interaction question here.)	
9. (Add specific skill-related questions here.)	
10. Is there anything you would like to add that we haven't discussed?	

Additional Notes:

Table 4.2 **Evaluation** Based on the candidate's responses, please provide a rating for each of the following categories:	
Skill	**Rating 1–4**
Ability to clearly communicate responsibilities and hold employees accountable	

Skill	Rating 1–4
Effective work style for the needs of the organization Examples may include: • Collaborative • Technically competent • Results-oriented • Cultural fit	
Experience that matches role	
Ability to address and solve problems appropriately	
Self-motivated	
Self-aware of both strengths and weaknesses	
Motivated to continue to develop and learn	
Ability to assess situations and make effective decisions	
Total Score	

Recommendation for Position:

____ Yes ____ No

Rating Scale

Rating	Definition
1	Not effective
2	Somewhat effective
3	Effective
4	Highly effective

Tables 4.3 and 4.4 are a sample interview guide and evaluation form for a leadership role that can be used to introduce or enhance your behavioral interviewing process.

Table 4.3 **Sample Interview Guide—Leadership**	
Candidate:	
Interviewer:	
Date:	

Question	Response
1. Please tell me how you define the role of (insert title here).	
2. Tell me about your management style. Please give me an example of how your management style has enabled you to be successful. Please tell me about a time when your style has not been effective.	
3. Please give me an example of a difficult employee issue that you have had to deal with. What was the outcome? Give me an example of a complex operations challenge and how you approached it.	
4. Tell me about your process for setting goals and holding yourself and your team accountable for achieving those goals.	
5. What are your career goals? Where are you relative to those goals, and what specifically are you doing to achieve them?	
6. How do you define the customers of this role or function?	

Question	Response
7. Please share both a positive and a negative customer interaction that you have had recently.	
8. (Add additional questions here.)	
9. Is there anything you would like to add that we haven't discussed?	

Additional Notes:

Table 4.4 **Evaluation** Based on the candidate's responses, please provide a rating for each of the following categories:	
Skill	**Rating 1–4**
Ability to clearly communicate responsibilities and hold employees accountable	
Effective management style for the needs of the organization Examples may include: • Participative • Open-door policy • Results-oriented • Cultural fit	
Experience in managing a wide range of employee challenges	
Ability to address and solve complex problems	
Self-motivated	
Self-aware of both strengths and weaknesses	
Motivated to continue to develop and learn	
Ability to assess situations and make effective decisions	
Total Score	

Recommendation for Position:

____ Yes ____ No

Rating Scale

Rating	Definition
1	Not effective
2	Somewhat effective
3	Effective
4	Highly effective

Everyone Wants to Weigh In

An increasing trend in the interview process has been to include almost everyone who can or will participate in the interviewing of a candidate. While there are certain benefits to having a wide range of opinions on a new hire decision, it is not without its challenges. We have heard of group interviews that felt like the Spanish Inquisition, with a panel of 8 or 10 interviewers and one interviewee! Not only is this intimidating for the candidate, but it becomes ineffective for the interviewers, as their particular roles in the process are not always clear. Will that many people actually be making or influencing the decision? Will some of the participants show their lack of enthusiasm for the process and have a negative impact on the group's impression of the candidate? It is critical to define who will actually participate in the interview process and what each person will contribute.

Suggested individuals to consider inviting to your interviews include:

- Recruiter

- Hiring manager

- HR business partner

- Peers

- Selected senior leader(s)

- Selected direct reports

- Selected internal clients

- Selected key stakeholders

Note: When using panels or group interviews, it is best not to exceed four or five internal participants. Always schedule time before the group interview to discuss the group members' individual roles, and reserve time following the interview to debrief them and discuss the next steps.

TIPS AND TAKEAWAYS FROM THIS CHAPTER

- Take every opportunity to "always be interviewing."

- Stay connected with your personal network.

- Keep up with talent and industry trends.

- Prepare your interview team and clarify its members' roles.

CHAPTER 5

Teaching Them
to Fish

Getting managers engaged and active in the talent selection and onboarding processes is critical. After all, they are the ones who have the most skin in the game when it comes to talent. These leaders' success is dependent on the people on their teams and their ability to perform. However, many of these managers are not engaged or active in the process. They continue to be distracted by the day-to-day operations of the business, and because they may not see themselves as being good at talent selection, they quickly opt out and delegate this responsibility to someone else. Because of HR's experience with this work and the fact that HR professionals are generally responsible for managing the administration of it, they get stuck with all or most of the work.

Meet Them Where They Are

The secret to getting managers engaged and really involved in the recruiting, hiring, and onboarding of your talent is to "meet them where they are." What we mean by this is that the human resources partner needs to take the time to understand what particular challenges managers are facing with regard to their business objectives, their current talent gaps, their prior experience with Human Resources (both positive and negative), their leadership style, and their personal development needs.

Here are some questions that the recruiting partner should answer to get a sense of the current state of the hiring manager:

- What do I know about this manager?

- How long has he or she been in this position?

- What do I know about his or her background?

- What type of reputation does he or she have in the organization?

- What has this manager's experience with HR been like?

- What do this manager's employees say about him or her?

- What type of communication does this manager prefer?

- What is important to this manager? And what are his or her "hot buttons"?

Getting to know the managers you support will serve you well as you work to support your organization by selecting and hiring the right talent. The benefits for both the managers and the recruiters are many. Managers will save time and resources by interviewing and considering only the best-fit candidates for their openings, and recruiters will also be more efficient and have a higher success rate of placements when they are highly aligned with their business partners.

Help Me Help You

It is often still a challenge to get good partnership between the managers of an organization and the recruiting team. Certainly there are often valid reasons for this disconnect, but it does not have to be that way. In fact, strong relationships and open, honest communications create better results for both the manager and the recruiter. Companies get better applicants if the hiring manager communicates the requirements clearly, and new hires "stick" better if recruiters have a good sense of what it is really like to work for that manager and that department. There are many more benefits for managers who take the time to get to know their recruiting partners because the recruiters can keep a "warm pipeline" of potential employees if they are closely connected to that part of the business and have a clear understanding of that manager's particular talent needs.

Relationships take time and energy, so the best strategy is a simple one:

- *Recruiters.* Make time to meet regularly with your client managers, and come with some knowledge of the business so that they can see that you are invested.

- *Managers.* Think of your recruiting partners as part of your operations team and invite them to participate in staff meetings, strategy sessions, goal-setting workshops, and social outings. The better they understand your department or function, the better they will recruit for you.

Once there is an open position available and the selection process is about to begin, there should always be a formal conversation between the person who will be leading the recruiting process and the hiring manager. Table 5.1 is a tool to add to your tool kit that will help you collect the information that will align the recruiter and the hiring manager so that they can successfully set up the process for selecting and hiring.

Recruiters may use this form to facilitate a discussion with the hiring manager concerning the key skills, competencies, and experiences that a potential candidate must have to be considered for the open role.

Prior to this interview, the recruiter should familiarize himself or herself with the role (that is, the job description, history of the position, and so on), the current state of this business unit or function, and this particular hiring manager.

Table 5.1 **Prehire Discussion Guide for Recruiting and Hiring Managers** Here are some suggested questions to ask the hiring manager:	
Question	**Notes**
Tell me about the position: • Newly created • Existing Tell me about its recent history: • Predecessor • Team overview	
	(continues)

Table 5.1 **Prehire Discussion Guide for Recruiting and Hiring Managers** *(continued)* Here are some suggested questions to ask the hiring manager:	
Question	**Notes**
What are the "must have" skills, competencies, and experience for this role? A particular background? Education? Previous employment?	
What are the "nice to haves" for this role?	
What specific technical skills are required? What soft skills?	
What are the key goals and objectives for the first year?	

Table 5.1 **Prehire Discussion Guide for Recruiting and Hiring Managers** (continued) Here are some suggested questions to ask the hiring manager:	
Question	**Notes**
What kind of person has been successful in this role? What kind has been unsuccessful?	
How do you envision us partnering or working together to fill this role?	

Unfortunately, there are still those managers who are just "too busy" and think that talent selection is all up to HR. One recruiter even describes this as managers who "don't want to get their hands dirty" by getting into the recruiting. There is also the flip side to this: hiring managers who are overinvolved and need to be included in every conversation and decision. What is common to both, this experienced recruiter says, is that they both want to know "why I don't have 10 (or fill in your own number here) candidates to look at." Managers typically think that re-cruiters have a stash of candidates that they can magically pull out whenever a job becomes available. Experienced talent selection professionals tell us that one of the ironies of having so much information available on the web is that this information makes it easier for potential candidates to say no to exploring job opportunities. They have access to information on websites like Glassdoor, where they can read postings from current or former employees of hun-dreds of organizations and decide whether they want to pursue anything there. LinkedIn, with its more than 259 million members, can connect anyone with some-one who can give inside information about what's like to work at any given company. Recruiters for companies with less-than-desirable employment brands or ones that are unknown have to work hard to sell their companies and get the attention of the talent that they want to attract.

Both managers and talent selection teams can benefit by staying connected to the top social media sites that to-day's job seekers are using. Table 5.2 is a quick checklist to share with your team.

Table 5.2	**Stay Connected for Talent Selection: A Checklist for Hiring Managers and Recruiting**		
Website	**Manager**	**Recruiter**	**Strategies for Use**
LinkedIn	√	√	• Maintain updated profiles • Post discussion topics • Join groups • Add contacts
Facebook	√	√	• Maintain updated profiles • Add friends • Post status, updates, and so on • Like pages/companies
Twitter	√	√	• Create accounts • Tweet—post messages with relevant info • Follow people and organizations in your target areas
The Ladders		√	• Maintain corporate account • Post job openings • Participate in discussions
Glassdoor	√	√	• Maintain corporate account • Read postings about your company • Read postings about your competitors • Post job openings • Participate in discussions
Indeed.com		√	• Maintain corporate account • Post job openings • Participate in discussions
Beyond.com		√	• Maintain corporate account • Post job openings • Participate in discussions
Executive Search Online		√	• Maintain corporate account • Post job openings • Participate in discussions

(continues)

Table 5.2 **Stay Connected for Talent Selection: A Checklist for Hiring Managers and Recruiting** *(continued)*			
Website	Manager	Recruiter	Strategies for Use
Snagajob.com (for hourly and part-time)		√	• Maintain corporate account • Post job openings • Participate in discussions
LinkUp		√	• Maintain corporate account • Post job openings • Participate in discussions
Monster	√	√	• Maintain corporate account • Create individual account • Read and comment on blogs • Post job openings • Participate in discussions

What's in It for Me?

Determining and describing what your hiring managers can gain from a strong partnership with the talent selection team is really the key to unlocking success—the "what's in it for me" (WIIFM). By clearly spelling out what the specific benefits to the hiring manager are, you will gain that manager's buy-in and support. If the benefit is only compliance with an internal process, there is a good chance that things will not change or improve. Another strategy is to "squeeze the pain"—that is, pinpoint what the manager's biggest talent selection concerns are and then offer a solution. Here are a few pain points for hiring managers:

- Too few qualified applicants

- Length of time required to fill positions

- Salary gaps between applicants and budget

- Bad fit of new hires

- Too much time to productivity for new hires

Using the prehire discussion guide will help you identify what your hiring managers' must-haves and nice-to-haves are for their open positions and will also give you information to help build your relationship.

On the other side of the coin, we know that considering the whole person is also critical. The practice of "mindful" onboarding gives HR leaders and managers tools for guiding precious talent to the next higher level of human potential. Mindfulness in the workplace is trending fast and hard. So we went to a California expert on how this practice is transforming the global business landscape.

Mindfulness Is the New Defining Quality in Potential Employee Selection and Onboarding

We invited subject-matter expert Dawa Tarchin Phillips, president and CEO of Empowerment Holdings, to share some of his

(continues)

expertise and insights on mindfulness and how it ties into on-boarding practices. Anne visited Dawa in his Santa Barbara offices to find out more about how his leadership develop-ment and consulting firm provides mindfulness-based lead-ership training and professional skills and interventions to businesses all over the world.

The Transforming Business Landscape

Insightful HR professionals, recruiters, talent management professionals, supervisors, managers, and attentive leaders can read the handwriting on the wall regarding the chang-ing recruitment landscape: The demand is increasing for high-quality, multifaceted, experienced talent in an in-creasingly competitive, fragmented, shifting, and individ-ualized economy.

The next generation of managers and talent scouts need to tap into this emerging trend—hiring employees who can stand firm and weather the changing seas and twisting tides of a transforming economy—if for no other reason than for its effects on people, organizations, and in-dustries. But what makes an employee stand out at effec-tive decision making, skillful communication, and coping with stressful events?

How can managers find talent that is resilient, confident, competent, and good at problem solving and that has increased focus and concentration? Why do some workers exhibit fewer antisocial behaviors and more organizational citizenship, seek greater learning, and display increased job satisfaction and organizational commitment?

What could be responsible for reducing negative attitudes, making less biased decisions, and having more realistic and accurate expectations? What holds the key to lower attrition rates as a result of less frustration and negative emotions, an increased ability to perform under stress, and a growing capacity for handling multiple demands?

According to Phillips, the qualities and competencies that read like a recruiter's wish list are grounded in the existing research on personnel who exhibit one significant trait over their equally talented competition: mindfulness.

Trending Now—Pocket Tool Kit Tips from Mindfulness Expert Dawa Tarchin Phillips

Mindfulness is not just another superfluous trend. Scientific literature on the matter is growing by the hour.

From reduced negative mood and attitude to increased optimism toward goal achievement, greater

(continues)

positive emotions and life satisfaction, and overall well-being and social connectedness, it's established that trait and state mindfulness bring an increase in the things that make people connect and thrive, while concurrently reducing stress, depression, rogue hostility, and aggression.

Research validates the effects of mindfulness on brain plasticity—that is to say, the act of being mindful of your thoughts actually connects to changes in your brain's activity and structure. These insights suggest that such changes in the brain help people experience improved focus, attention, life skill, satisfaction, and well-being, and reduce mental, emotional, and physical distress—all as a result of choosing to change how we think!

With so much data and grounded argument making this case, isn't it time for business professionals to take a closer look and consider identifying some of these important and timely characteristics in talent selection and recruitment?

Is your workforce mindful? Are you screening for mindfulness? Are you empowering your personnel with the tools and programs they need if they are to cultivate this intentional and universal panacea?

Before answering these questions, it might be helpful to assess your own mindfulness to gain a more intimate understanding of what it can offer you and your organization.

Cultivate Discernment

You can start to explore what mindfulness is and how it can affect your everyday interactions by following these four short reflections:

- Investigate and acknowledge that what you control in your life boils down to what you think, imagine, say, and do and how you **choose** to respond to life's daily events and challenges.

- Investigate and acknowledge that all these things take place during the present moment experience, each day, every day.

- Investigate and acknowledge that if you are not present in this moment, you subsequently have little or no control in your life right now.

- Resolve that well-intended attempts to gain greater control by not being fully present are not only irrational but generally counterproductive.

(continues)

Next, you can take steps and develop a few disciplines that make being present easier and being mindful feel natural.

Here are a few easy steps that might lend themselves to being talking points during your next recruiting session or while trying to enroll a leader of the next generation.

- *Cultivate mindfulness every day.* Do this consciously and by choice. Like compounding interest, it will pay you back handsomely over time. The value and benefit of five minutes of practice today grows exponentially, and will pay you back multifold over a year, five years, or a lifetime. Here is how to start:

  - *Sit or stand in an upright posture.* Find a comfortable seat or posture that allows you to have a straight spine, which quickly translates into greater mental clarity and allows you to stay alert longer without becoming drowsy or dull.

  - *Connect with your physical sensations.* Whether you are walking, standing, sitting, or lying down, connect with your physical sensations in the present moment. This not only grounds you, but also strengthens your empathy because the awareness of your own physical sensations helps you relate more to those around you.

- *Cultivate trust.* Nothing distracts and clouds the mind like ongoing worry and anxiety. Choose to cultivate trust instead. Invest in your ability to be human and simply do your best; don't pursue delusions of grandeur, deny your own vulnerability, or hate yourself for your own human imperfections.

- *"Anchor" your attention.* Focus on your breath, your sensations, or simply a spot on the wall; anchor your attention in the present moment for minutes at a time by returning again and again to the object of your training.

- *Cultivate nonjudgment.* Also called openness or acceptance, this is the decision and ability to suspend self-judgment on your own present mental and emotional state. Shift your focus to fully being with your own state, as it is.

- *Cultivate kindness.* Kindness can be summarized as a commitment to not abusing yourself or others for the sake of money, image, or status, but to engage

(continues)

in big-picture thinking that sees your own well-being aligned with that of those around you.

The simple truth of these reflections can help you access your own full potential and that of your people. In order to be great at what you do, you first need to be here to do it.

Phillips is also a research specialist at the Department of Psychological and Brain Sciences at UC Santa Barbara and the founder and executive director of the Institute of Compassionate Awareness. For more information on specific training tools and presentations worldwide regarding this subject, contact Dawa at dtp@empowermentholdings.com or 805-680-3988 or visit www.empowermentholdings.com.

The Harvard Challenge

Harvard professor of management practice Bill George knows firsthand what the power of mindfulness can mean to a leader's role in any organization. The former Honeywell and Medtronic executive created an elective for Harvard's curriculum called "Authentic Leadership Development."

According to George, the important practice of mindfulness tools, as Phillips describes, helps employees to measure and manage life as they are living it. In a *Harvard Business Review* blog, George says that mindfulness teaches us to pay attention to the present moment, recognize feelings and emotions, and practice keeping them under control, especially in high-stress work environments and situations.

Harvard is challenging its students to redefine their definition of success and to consider the impact of truly making a positive difference in the lives of their colleagues, their companies, and their friends and families.

George says, "When you are mindful, you are aware of your presence and the ways you affect people. You observe and participate in every moment." In today's workplace, these are requisites if you are to truly improve performance, productivity, and employee confidence and to get the job done.

Follow-Through Formula: DWYSYGD (Do What You Say You're Gonna Do)

The last and maybe the most important component of getting managers engaged and involved in the talent selection process is that the talent selection team must deliver what it has committed to as well. Nothing disengages a manager more than a partner who does not hold up his or her end of the deal. Just as the HR business partners must prove themselves in a way by understanding the operational challenges of the organization and being able to offer talent solutions to them, those on the talent acquisition team must do the same. They will gain credibility with the company leaders they support if they demonstrate deep knowledge and understanding of the business objectives and then are able to support them by delivering top talent to fill their open positions.

TIPS AND TAKEAWAYS FROM THIS CHAPTER

- Do your homework—understand your hiring managers.

- Create the business case and WIIFM.

- Put the time into maintaining your relationship with your managers.

- Deliver what you promise.

CHAPTER 6

They're In: Now What?

What Is Onboarding?

Since the mid-1990s, onboarding has been "on the radar" of most HR managers inside larger organizations. Michael Watkins in his book *The First 90 Days* made onboarding a relevant business topic, and many organizations followed his lead and created onboarding experiences for their new hires. Unfortunately, however, these experiences varied wildly and had mixed results. Some organizations defined onboarding as something similar to orientation, whereas others left it to the new hires themselves and provided little or no organizational support.

The following definition of onboarding has evolved and worked best for our clients:

> Onboarding is a structured process, lasting between three and six months, that positions an organization's new employees with the organization's vision, strategies, goals, and culture. It integrates the new employee into the organization, business unit or function, and role. Successful onboarding experiences are a partnership of the new employees, their managers, and human resources partners.[1]

Onboarding plays an important role as a key program that should take place between the recruitment (or talent selection) process and the performance management program in an organization. Onboarding is the "bridge" between the résumé screening, interviewing, and selection of a job candidate and the annual review measuring how well that employee is doing in her or his job.

Onboarding Versus Orientation

Our definition of onboarding highlights the key differences between onboarding and orientation. A typical orientation is event-based (lasting only hours in some cases or at most one or two days) and is a one-way communication that is generally not tailored to meet all of a new hire's needs. Its purpose is to meet the basic needs of a broad range of new employees and provide a setting for trans-actions related to starting a new job. Onboarding is a longer-term program that is designed specifically for a particular new hire and his or her role but that also pro-vides a consistent experience for all who are onboarding in the organization. Its focus is on speeding the learning pro-cess and supporting higher-level performance.

Table 6.1 is a quick reference guide to the differences between a typical orientation and an onboarding experience.

Table 6.1 **Quick Reference Guide: Orientation Versus Onboarding**	
Orientation	**Onboarding**
Purpose: To provide new employees with baseline information about the organization and complete the new hire paperwork. It usually occurs in a classroom setting as an event and is facilitated by the HR function.	*Purpose:* To provide new employees with the opportunity to gain knowledge, build relationships, and act on feedback for the purpose of successfully and quickly integrating into the organization. It usually occurs over the first 90 days of employment and is facilitated by the hiring manager and the HR partner.
• Single event	• Process lasts for the first three to six months
• One-way information flow to the new hires	• Information flows through several channels, to and from the new hires
• "One-size-fits-all" process	• Customized by function and role
• Human Resources—led	• Human Resources/Employee Development—facilitated; new hire and hiring manager participate *(continues)*

Table 6.1 **Quick Reference Guide:** Orientation Versus Onboarding *(continued)*	
Orientation	**Onboarding**
• Logistical and tactical	• Integrative and strategic
• Organizational overview information delivered to a group	• Functional and role-specific information delivered "just in time" and on the job
• Classroom-style learning	• Blended learning approach
• One-way exposure of information about the organizational culture	• "Live and learn" the organizational culture, while getting feedback
• Associates are still "new" after orientation	• Associates have fully made the transition to the organization, culture, and role after onboarding

A Virtual Packet

What types of information should you provide to your new employees, and how much? How should it be delivered? As you consider building out this phase of the onboarding program, think about what your new employees have said that they wished they had known when they first started. Are there important parts of your culture that you want to reinforce? Is your organizational structure complex and hard to understand? Do you have a story about your history that is important for everyone to know? These are the common pieces of knowledge that all employees, regardless of level or function, should have about your organization, and they can be delivered easily and inexpensively with e-mail and links to your website.

First, decide what you are going to communicate. Perhaps you should provide:

- Links to company website pages

- Current press releases

- Recent presentations and internal communications

- Welcome messages from the company's leaders

- Videos or photos of company events

- Links to resources or information about the community

- Relocation resources

- What to expect next—orientation, onboarding, and Week 1 activities

Next, decide when you will communicate this information. It is a good idea to break up the communication into at least two different parts, maybe using two different methods of communication. For example, send one e-mail with the links to information and then follow up with a phone call. If there is time and opportunity, send an additional e-mail before the new employee's first day to confirm and link everyone together.

Then, with a simple e-mail template, either the hiring manager or the HR partner can send these communications with clear and consistent content. Figure 6.1 is an example of e-mail templates that you can use for your first and second prestart communications.

Figure 6.1 **E-mail Templates for First and Second Prestart Communications**

First Prestart E-mail

Hello _____,

Congratulations on your new role of _____ here at (Company/Division)! We are looking forward to working with you.

It is important to us that you get off to a great start here at (Company). We understand that beginning a new role in a new organization is both exciting and a little overwhelming. I will be working with you and (manager) to provide you with the information and support that you need to be successful.

As you know, becoming familiar with the (Company) culture is an important part of your transition. I have attached a few articles and links to resources that will build on the information you gained during the interview process.

[Suggested links or attachments:]

- *Recent newsletters*

- *E-mail messages from the CEO or other key leaders*

- *Community involvement and/or philanthropic information*

- *Any other recent events or documents that demonstrate the organizational culture*

Please let me know if you have any questions regarding any of the information attached. I will be in touch with you prior to your start date to review your first week's agenda and answer any questions you may have. Do not hesitate to contact me at any time.

Sincerely,

(HR partner or hiring manager)

Second Prestart E-mail

Hello _____!

I wanted to touch base with you as we approach your start date on (date) to review your first week's agenda and logistics. Your first week will be a combination of orientation, meet and greet meetings, and general setup. I will be meeting with

(continues)

you on (date) to discuss how I will support you during your transition.

The orientation program will cover:

- *Overall company information*

- *Benefit information and enrollment*

- *(Add content)*

Day 1 Logistics:

- *Please park in the (section name) of the parking lot.*

- *Ask for (name) at the front desk. He or she will take you to your office.*

I look forward to seeing you soon! Please feel free to call or e-mail me with any questions that you may have.

Sincerely,

(Name)

The most critical thing about the prestart phase is that there is two-way communication between the new employee and the organization. We have seen companies lose new people during the prestart period when there is a gap in communication. The organization didn't realize that the new employee was having doubts about accepting the position or was being pursued by another company, and then the new hire never makes it to Day 1.

We Love Onboarding Logistics (Not Really, but They're Important)

One of the things we are constantly reminding our clients is that organizations do not get credit for doing the logistical parts of onboarding correctly, but when these areas are done badly, their new employees will remember it. There are thousands of stories that get told and retold about employees showing up for their first day of work and having no desk, computer, phone, or other essential thing that they need if they are to be productive or feel as though the organization expected them on the first day. There is even a story from Louis Gerstner Jr. in his book *Who Says Elephants Can't Dance?* how, as the newly selected president of IBM, he was locked out of his office building on the first day and had to bang on the door and convince a suspicious housekeeper to let him in! Mr. Gerstner's staff suffered the embarrassment of that mistake, but the organization learned an important onboarding lesson.

Companies that pay attention to the logistical details of their onboarding process can take these items off the table and allow their new hires to focus on what they were hired to do. Not only are logistical mistakes embarrassing, but they are distractions, and a new hire's speed to becoming productive can be really negatively affected.

How can you address your logistical issues so that they are nonissues? We suggest that you create a logistics checklist and include all the key partners in your organization, while giving ownership to one key individual to execute the checklist every time a new hire starts. This logistics checklist will make sure that you have captured everything that your new employee will need. This will also help you identify where the processes may be broken and need to be reviewed. Table 6.2 is an example of a logistics checklist that you can customize for your organization.

Table 6.2 **Logistics Checklist**				
Item	Resource Contact	Number	Date Expected	Date Completed
Office location identified, furnished, and set up				
Phone (with password) connected				
Mobile phone purchased and set up				
Computer, laptop, and/or tablet equipment ordered and in place				
Connected to company network				
E-mail address set up				

Table 6.2 **Logistics Checklist** *(continued)*				
Item	Resource Contact	Number	Date Expected	Date Completed
Business cards completed and in the office				
Basic office supplies				
Application for company credit card				
Nameplate for office				
Company phone directory				
Organization charts				
Temporary discount card prepared				
Schedule for orientation session (if applicable)				
Travel expense reimbursement documents				
Travel profile				
Travel policy book				
Relocation expense reimbursement documents				
ID and/or security badge				
Office keys				
Tour of building				
Appropriate policy and procedures manuals				
HR information: Payroll Benefits				

Unfortunately, you usually don't get credit for doing all the logistical preparation correctly and on time, but you certainly will hear about it if any part of it is not done correctly or on time. It is amazing how much of a distraction these "small things" can be for a new hire, a manager, or HR if they are done hastily or inaccurately. We know of one department head who had her medical benefits delayed for two months because of a paperwork error and who was so preoccupied with this issue that she couldn't talk to her HR partner about anything else until it was resolved. This led to the new leader's not being convinced that HR could get anything right, and she was labeled as "high maintenance" by the organization. Avoidable? Absolutely! Create the list, make the assignments, and build in checkpoints to make sure that everything is complete or to handle issues as they surface.

By using a formal and consistent checklist, you can ensure that your new hires have what they need to hit the ground running on Day 1. This is the story that they will tell their family and friends that will strengthen your organization's employment brand.

Getting Everyone Else Ready

In most organizations, it is pretty typical for there to be an announcement of some kind when a new person joins the organization. This is usually in an e-mail, and its distribution often depends on the level and position of that individual (in some companies, the e-mail always goes to everyone). The mistake that most organizations make with this type of broad communication is that they stop there. They assume that they have communicated who the new person is and why he or she is being hired, so they're done. Wrong! Additional and more targeted communication is needed for a couple of different groups.

First, does the new hire have people who are direct reports? A separate communication to the team, preferably a face-to-face one, should take place. Next, are there key people who have a stake in the new hire's success, such as internal or external clients, vendors and suppliers, peers, or anyone else? Additional communication with them is also needed, and they should also be invited to participate in the initial *personal network* meetings of the new hire. These are often also called "meet and greet" meetings, but unfortunately, they tend to lack structure and purpose. However, if done correctly, these meetings can be a jump start for a new employee as she or he begins to build relationships. Figure 6.2 is an example of how to get your personal network meetings successfully launched.

Figure 6.2 **E-mail Template to All Invitees in
New Hire's Personal Network**

Hello_____,

As you know, (new hire's name) will be joining our team soon. As part of his/her onboarding, he/she will be meeting with several members of our team and organization. To help you prepare for the meeting, we have outlined suggested agenda items to make the most of your time with (new hire's name).

As you know, this is a very important part of the (new hire's name) time here at (Company). Personal network meetings allow the new hire to begin to build relationships and continue to learn more about our organization and how we work.

Suggested agenda items for this important meeting:

- *Discuss the new hire's background.*

- *Share your background both at (Company) and any previous experience.*

- *Provide an overview of your role and your team.*

- *Discuss how your team and the new hire's team interact.*

- *Share your thoughts on how effectively the team members currently work together.*

> • *Ask the new leader how he or she is experiencing the culture.*
>
> • *Identify specific follow-up items.*
>
> • *Agree to any next steps.*
>
> *Please let me know if you have any questions, and thank you for your participation!*
>
> *Sincerely,*
>
> *(Name)*

Cover All Orientation Bases

A new hire's first week on the job is exciting, long, and overwhelming. It can also be confusing, frustrating, and boring if it is not planned and carried out well. Many organizations start their new employees off with a formal orientation. Such an orientation is defined differently by each organization. For larger, mature organizations, orientation usually means a formal, classroomlike experience for its new hires that can last from a few hours to a few days. This program often includes the processing of new hire paperwork and a review of the company's policies and procedures. It can also include videos or presentations of the company history, an introduction to its culture, and highlights or overviews of its core business and results. The audience for this type of orientation is usually fairly broad and includes new hires at various levels and in various functions, departments, or even business units of the organizations. So, the content must also be fairly broad to fit this wider audience, and that creates a challenge for both the organization and the new hires. If a disproportionate amount of orientation time is spent on topics that are too broad and are not connected to the roles of the individuals who are participating, the organization loses the chance to connect with those individuals and show them how they individually will be able to contribute to the organization's results. Often, new leaders are the first to "check out" and either disengage from the program (take calls, check e-mails, and the like) or not attend it at all. This is especially true if orientation involves a large group that includes both exempt and nonexempt new hires of various levels. Some organizations require all their new hires to attend these sessions and state that the benefits include the opportunities to interact with people in the organization that you may not have the chance to interact with in your job. Again, if the organization is purposeful about this and gets constant feedback from its participants indicating that it is working, orientation can be a great tool to promote the desired culture and behaviors in an organization.

In smaller, newer, or decentralized organizations, orientation can also involve sitting in a conference room with an HR partner filling out forms or reporting directly to the new work area and working one-on-one with the hiring manager. This type of orientation is not necessarily wrong or bad, but it can miss some key elements, and it is usually inconsistent. One of the strongest parts of a business case for a larger, more centralized orientation is that it can deliver information to the new hires consistently and in an efficient and effective way. However, in smaller or decentralized organizations, a common orientation is not cost-effective. So, often HR will provide some basic tools and resources, and the management team in the department, function, or business unit can deliver the important information to the new hire during his or her first days on the job.

TIPS AND TAKEAWAYS FROM THIS CHAPTER

- Orientation is a one-way, one-time, one-size-fits-all activity.

- Onboarding is long-term, is role-specific, and supports two-way information flow.

- Get your logistics right the first time around.

- Address the new hire's personal networks.

- Establish how and to whom the basics of your orientation program will be targeted.

CHAPTER 7

Don't Lose Them— Wow Them!

Are You Experienced?

N o one wants to feel that he or she is just going through a "process"—especially new leaders and new hires with high expectations. Today, new hires expect companies to be prepared for them when they arrive, and they expect a more formal transition period. New leaders do not want to sit through a day's worth of presentations about ID badges, attendance policies, and benefits administration. Your new hires need information that will help them understand your organization's business processes, culture, and people. By offering a structured onboarding program, organizations have an advantage when competing for top talent.

When your organization creates a best-practice onboarding experience, it says to your new hires that:

- We are expecting you.

- We care about you and are excited about your decision to join us.

- We want to help you be successful.

- We are focused on you.

It is really important to tie the onboarding experience to your culture and your story—again, make the connection to drive the engagement of all your new hires in each of the generational groups.

Grab Them from the Start

Studies show that employee engagement is at its highest when the employee first accepts the job and is in the *prestart* phase of onboarding.

> Prestart: The period that begins upon a candidate's acceptance of a new job and continues until her or his first day on the job.

As new hires get ready to start a new role, they are disconnecting from their current role and/or organization and are anxious to gain as much information as possible about the new one. Connecting early and often is even more important for your millennial new hires, who may be weighing multiple job offers. An organization that takes advantage of the prestart period will win the hearts and minds of this talent pool, according to several recruiters we know. These new hires want to belong to a community and start to form relationships with their manager and peers, not just wait to report to a job on Day 1.

- Does the new hire hear from his or her hiring manager after acceptance and before the start date?

- Does the company send an information packet or link to the company website or onboarding landing page?

- Does the new hire know what to expect once he or she has accepted?

Use inexpensive and easy ways (onboarding landing page, e-mail, texts, LinkedIn, Facebook, Twitter, and the like) to connect with your newest talent. Videos, photos, and links can also be an effective way to communicate with your new hires. Don't disappoint them!

Prestart for Leaders is Different

New leaders' prestart experiences are where you can have the biggest impact with both integration of the new hire into the culture and the jump start of building key relationships. We strongly encourage as much contact as possible between the new leader, her manager, peers, and the HR partner between offer acceptance and Day 1. Managers should take the opportunity to meet for lunch, dinner, or coffee and have a different kind of conversation from the recruiting ones. New leaders can start to check out their peers in a more casual setting and get to know them as people before they are deep into the business issues that they will face together shortly. Our experience is that if this time and energy is committed in the prestart phase, the new leader can truly "hit the ground running" much more easily than if all these initial introductions are left to happen in the first few weeks on the job. The message that this sends to the new leader is that the organization cares enough about her transition and understanding of the culture to invest the time. Early impressions and interactions on both sides can set the stage for success or failure for new leaders. Organizations that understand and act on this will impress their new leaders and help them know that they made the right decision in joining their organization.

On the flip side, if a new leader shows interest and initiative in these prestart activities, the organization will most likely feel that it also made the right choice and it will start to reap the benefits of that hire before she sets foot in the office.

Suggested prestart activities for leaders include:

- Lunch or coffee with the manager

- Casual meetings with peers, direct reports, or other key people

- Access to the company intranet, social media, and regular conference calls

- Attendance at "special" meetings (quarterly briefing, stockholders' meeting, all-employee meeting, holiday celebration etc.)

- Participation in community and charity events

Who's Wowing Their New Employees

- **SAS:** The company has an onsite health center that is open to all family members. It has more than 50 medical and support staff, including nurse

(continues)

practitioners, family practice physicians, dietitians, psychologists, and physical therapists.

- *General Mills, Microsoft, and Nordstrom:* Efforts by these companies helped to legalize same-sex marriage in Minnesota and Washington.

- *The Container Store:* Getting ready for its IPO last year, this retailer reserved an unprecedented percentage of shares for its employees to purchase. A quarter of the employees bought stock, and the share price doubled on the first day of trading, from $18 to $36.

- *Qualcomm:* Awards to employees make this a happy workplace—$1,500 bonuses for filing a new patent went to more than 1,700 employees last year!

- *Southwest Airlines:* New hires are matched up with a mentor "buddy" during their first week on the job. Each buddy is expected not only to follow the Southwest onboarding program with his or her new hire buddy but also to purchase "out of pocket" a few small gifts (usually Southwest-branded items) to make the new hire feel welcome and part of the team. The idea is that the mentor buddy's paying for these items represents his or her personal investment in the new employee and his or her commitment to the organization. Wow!

Techno Rules

We have found that using technology in appropriate ways can best support your onboarding's consistency and scalability objectives. The easier and more accessible you make your onboarding program to your new hires and hiring managers, the more they will use it. One of our specialty retail clients' main onboarding objectives for using a web-based solution was to get its onboarding "off all the Excel spreadsheets" that were circulating in the company. The spreadsheets contained information and content that varied by function, department, and manager, so they were not able to leverage all the collective organizational and departmental knowledge that the organization had. The organization offered no consistency in what its new hires were experiencing. When everything was moved to the web, the company intelligence was stable, up to date, and available to all the people who needed to access it. The website delivery also made viewing and using the onboarding plan and its supporting resources a lot more interesting and engaging for the company's new hires. The organization also benefited from the perception that it was using best-practice onboarding methods delivered by current technology.

Possible items to put on an onboarding portal include:

- Current strategies or initiatives presentations

- Organization charts, e-mail directory, and leadership bios

- Job aids

- Company meeting notes

- Links to the company intranet

- Links to the learning management system

- Employee handbook

- Benefits information

- Company calendar

Power in Numbers

Onboarding your new hires in groups can be really effective and can produce great results. It allows new hires, especially new leaders, to bond with coworkers who are going through the same experiences and allows for interaction among different parts of the organization that otherwise might not occur. Strong and lasting relationships are formed that can significantly support driving business objectives. If you have a large, diverse organization, it is important that you create these onboarding groups thoughtfully. You may consider creating a leadership group (like director or vice president and above), a management group, and then an all-associates group. We recommend, however, that these groups be cross-functional to encourage networking and knowledge sharing across the organization.

Some suggested group onboarding activities are:

- Lunches, coffees, and happy hours for new hires hired within a certain time frame

- Workshops hosted by HR or other subject-matter experts and centered around common onboarding topics

- Brown-bag discussions on specified learning topics

Suggested onboarding topics for group meetings:

- *Role clarity.* Is this the role you expected based on the interview process?

- *Navigating the culture:* How is this culture different from what you expected?

- *Building relationships:* Which relationships have proven helpful with your onboarding, and which ones do you still need to develop?

- *Working with your manager:* How have you gotten to know your manager and how he or she prefers to work?

- *Getting feedback:* How does this organization provide feedback, and what are its expectations for acting on it?

- *Leadership culture:* What is expected of leaders, and what behaviors are important for success?

Bring in the Celebrities

Onboarding may be the only time when some of your new hires will get to meet and interact with your senior leadership team. Take advantage of your passionate, high-energy leaders and invite them to speak to a group of new associates at a coffee or lunch get-together. Let your leaders tell stories about their experiences in the organization and why they are excited to welcome these new associates. Ask them to share their advice about how to be successful in your organization.

At a conference we attended, one HR partner shared that her organization hosted dinners with the president every quarter so that new employees could hear him speak and ask him questions directly. She said that it was his commitment to these dinners and his passion for the business that shaped the familial culture that the organization enjoyed. Employees shared stories of these famous dinners, and some were able to develop personal relationships with the CEO after first meeting him there. Almost all of this company's employees were consistently highly engaged and loyal, and this HR partner was convinced that much of this success stemmed from how the company "grabbed people from the start."

Mentors Can Support the Wow!

Another popular way of raising the level of engagement of your new hires is to give leaders as mentors to key new talent. This will support several objectives for both the new hire and the leader: it gives the mentor an opportunity to help the new hire understand and learn how to be successful in the new culture, and it creates a development opportunity to enable the leader to improve his or her coaching skills. It is obvious, though, that not all leaders make good mentors. There are specific qualities to look for in your leaders when you are deciding whether they will be good mentors. Strong mentors must be highly self-aware, work continuously to understand others, and have the key communication skills of active listening, effective questioning, and giving feedback.

Beyond the typical information that all new hires need when they join an organization or get promoted to a new role, there is a great deal of learning and experience that high-potential new hires can get from a good mentor. It is important to be specific about what you want your mentors and mentees to focus on so that your new hires are experiencing consistency. Give your mentors a road map to follow and certain areas on which to focus their conversations with their mentees.

Here are some topics to consider having your mentors work on with their onboarding mentees:

- Understanding our strategy and strategy communication

- What trust means in our culture

- Our business model and business acumen

- A day in the life at (insert company name)

- Work/life balance and stress management

- Building strategic relationships

- Career development planning

- Continuous learning at (insert company name)

- Working cross-culturally

- Becoming a leader at (insert company name)

- Influencing others

- The power and impact of providing recognition

- Communicate! Communicate! Communicate!

Your mentors and your new hires will benefit from this structured yet flexible approach to partnership learning.

TIPS AND TAKEAWAYS FROM THIS CHAPTER

- Wow your new hires during prestart with several touch points.

- Build a consistent onboarding program for all your new hires.

- Use technology whenever possible.

- Include your senior leaders in onboarding.

- Sweat the small stuff and create a logistics checklist.

CHAPTER 8

Making Your Newest Employees Raving Fans

One of the best-kept secrets of employers who have no trouble attracting, hiring, and retaining top talent is that they use their new hires and their current candidate pool as recruiters. These organizations know how to leverage the experiences that job seekers have with their organization into a competitive advantage for attracting talent. Those organizations with consumer brands probably understand this best because they look at every interaction with people as an opportunity to expose those people to their brand and convert them into happy customers.

> ## Darden Restaurants' Employees Are Raving Fans
>
> More than half of the employees here donate to a special program that provides relief and assistance to fellow employees who are facing emergencies.

Everyone Has a Story

When was the last time you got great customer service? How about really terrible service? How many people did you tell about either of those experiences? Chances are that you told someone about both the good experience and the bad one (and you probably told more people about the bad experience). Similarly, we all have probably had either a terrific interviewing or hiring experience or a horrific one. Most of us will repeat the bad story many more times than the good one, but nonetheless these stories will be repeated, and today they will probably be shared via social media. Organizations that see touch points with potential employees as opportunities to create fans or customers of their brands are smart. They know that leveraging each and every interaction, whether it is active or passive, can make the difference in how they are viewed. Talent selection professionals know that candidates will share their stories widely, usually via social media, so it is really important to create as positive an experience as possible for them. Dozens, if not hundreds, of people will know what happened in a phone screening or a face-to-face interview minutes after it occurred, with your organization's name attached. Small things like how you explain your process, follow up when you say you are going to, and communicate openly and honestly can have a significant impact on how your organization will be viewed from the candidates' perspectives, and will also influence all their followers on the web. The most important thing is knowing what your newest employees are saying about you. Don't wait until someone posts something on Glassdoor or Facebook to find out; use the tool in Table 8.1 to seek feedback and make changes to improve your processes.

Table 8.1 Building an Onboarding Program
Interview Guide—Recently Hired Leaders or Associates

Name:	Position:	Start date:	Relo:	Today's date:

Question	Response
1. Please describe the recruitment and selection process that you experienced.	
2. What made you decide to join our organization?	

(continues)

Question *(continued)*	Response
3. Tell me about your role here. Is your role different from what you expected? If yes, how?	
4. Please describe your first week on the job. How did you spend your time, and what were your experiences?	
5. What role did your manager play during your first 90 days?	
6. What role did HR play during your first 90 days?	
7. What challenges did you face during your first 90 days?	
8. How did you go about understanding how to navigate the culture? How long did that take?	
9. Who or what did you rely on to help you in your first 90 days?	
10. What do you think our organization should do to help new leaders or associates successfully make the transition into the organization or community?	
11. Additional notes	

Develop on Day 1

There is a great deal of research that deals with an employee's "stickiness" to an organization (the likelihood that he or she will stay with that organization). Baby boomers are the group that is most associated with loyalty and tenure. Millennials want more than a job and a paycheck. They seek to be engaged and to have an opportunity to use and develop their skills. New information from the Wynhurst Group finds that employee turnover within the first 45 days on the job is actually 22 percent. So about one out of every four new employees leaves just after the first six weeks! This is not an acceptable number for most companies, and addressing it before it happens in your organization is critical. Some companies have embraced the idea of starting development on Day 1 by having conversations with the new hire about how and where he or she might progress in the organization. (Chapter 10 provides a case study on Volkswagen's relocation to Washington, DC.) This is especially important to the millennials, given the way they view the world. Their attitude is, "Everyone gets a trophy, and everyone gets promoted," and their ideal is that their expectations are aligned with the expectations and the real talent needs of the organization. Thus, talent selection and development professionals need to get out ahead and start to incorporate development during the onboarding phase. By including development objectives that came to the surface during the selection phase, managers of new hires can show that they are aware of these needs and are interested in helping new employees develop the skills that are necessary for future roles. Many organizations use formal assessment tools during interviewing to pinpoint specific development areas, whereas others rely on their experience and interviewing skills to detect this information. Either method is effective; however, the information provided should be shared and validated by the new employee in order to get buy-in that he or she is included in the onboarding plan.

Figure 8.1 is an example of an onboarding plan for a new leader that includes development objectives.

Figure 8.1 **Onboarding Plan for New Leaders**

Onboarding Plan, Month 1

Focus: Role clarity and organizational knowledge

Sample onboarding objectives

- Understand core competencies and processes of the organization.

- Understand the organization's language.

- Clarify role.

Developmental objective: Increase business acumen and understanding of competitive landscape

- Understand the organization's core values, strategic plan, and direction.

Connecting with your manager

- Meet with HR partner to address questions and concerns.

- Meet with manager to clarify role and to discuss progress on objectives and early wins.

Engaging with your team and stakeholders

- Meet with your team.

- Meet with stakeholders.

- Complete stakeholder analysis.

By creating specific objectives and tangible development goals, you will demonstrate to your new hires that you are committed to investing in them and want them to succeed. This will be the message that they communicate to their networks, and it will help to fill your pipeline with top talent for your organization. These new leaders and new employees will become the raving fans that you want to have representing you.

The Magic of Early Wins

Looking at the hundreds of new hires that we've seen in the many organizations that we've worked with, one of the surefire ways to engage them is to make them successful quickly. Especially for new leaders, the power of getting a few things done early and effectively is magical. The benefits are many for both the organization and the new hire. The new hire can actually do something productive in his or her first weeks on the job, and the organization can see the new hire "in action." This boosts the confidence of both the new person and his hiring manager and team. The danger, however, is that a new employee does not want to come on too strong or too fast, thereby sabotaging any future impact by trying to do too much too soon. The trick, then, is to plan and predict what are those "early wins" or "quick hits" that a new hire can complete that will gain him or her some momentum and traction in the new role without moving too fast and upsetting his or her ability to fit into the organizational culture.

Table 8.2 is a template to support the planning and execution of these early wins.

Note: This exercise is essential for all new leaders; it may not apply to all new individual contributor roles, but it should be considered nonetheless.

Table 8.2 Early Win Deliverables

To help you plan early win deliverables, understand their importance to the organization, and identify the resources needed for success in delivering those early wins, identify the half dozen initiatives or work products that could be used to gauge your effectiveness as a new leader over the first three to four months in your new position. Review this material with your human resources partner and hiring manager to align expectations and determine the appropriate resources.

Deliverable and Timing (and Related Expectations)	How It Supports Larger (or Longer-Term) New Leader Performance Objective	Resources Required
Example: Establish yourself as the leader and set the team direction	*Example:* Establishes leadership	*Example:* All members of the team

• Meet one-on-one with team members to get to know them on a personal and professional level (both direct and indirect reports)
  • Roles and areas of responsibility
  • Strengths
  • Areas to develop/provide coaching
  • Level of autonomy, direction, or support needed to enable direct reports to perform their responsibilities
• Begin or continue staff meetings
• Establish team norms and team alignment sessions
	Eases associates' apprehension
	
	Develops and/or strengthens relationships
	
	Leadership competencies connection: develops others, acts with integrity, and builds effective teams	

Rewards Are Nice, Too

Some organizations use incentives and rewards to encourage their employees to help them recruit and hire new talent. These programs do work, and the ones that work best are probably those that are designed to specifically target the most difficult-to-fill jobs and also have both immediate and long-term payback associated with them. Successful incentive programs tie a small but attractive reward (usually monetary, like $500) to the referral of a candidate with the right skill set for these jobs. If the candidate is converted to a new employee and stays with the organization for a minimum amount of time, the employee who initiated the referral gets another reward, usually larger (anywhere from $1,000 to a certain percentage of the role's salary). The program gives incentives both for serious referrals and for the stickiness of those employees with the organization. Organizations can also have success with programs that reward at a lower rate (say $50 gift cards) for attracting large numbers of a certain type of employee—for example, seasonal workers. The key to creating a successful rewards program is to match the reward with the objectives of the program, then clearly communicate the program to your employees.

If organizations stay engaged with their newest employees and don't simply "check the box" to indicate that another position has been filled, then they will benefit by being sought by top talent and not having to recruit as hard or as often, even for those tough-to-fill positions.

TIPS AND TAKEAWAYS FROM THIS CHAPTER

- Leverage your newest employees for recruiting.

- Find out what they are saying about you and manage it.

- Engage them from Day 1 with development and early wins.

- The onboarding plan has many applications—use them all.

- Use incentive programs for hard-to-fill positions.

CHAPTER 9

Onboarding with the Best of Them

I t is not a surprise that the "hottest" employers, those who are attracting the best and the brightest of the current talent pool, are also the ones that have put special emphasis on their onboarding experiences. However, there are also examples of companies that have been around for years that understand how important these first weeks and months on the job are for their new hires. They have stayed committed to onboarding and have programs that should be emulated.

Facebook Boot Camp

It's no secret that Facebook has been growing exponentially and having to hire highly sought-after software engineers at the same time as its tech competitors are trying to do the same. Four years ago, it created Facebook Boot Camp for its new hires. The boot camp model pairs new engineers with a mentor who gets them immersed in the social network's massive code base. The "boot campers" attend tech talks and get assigned tasks like fixing bugs, building internal tools, and upgrading software. The whole time, they and their work are reviewed by the mentor. After six weeks, the new hire gets to choose which team to join, with the idea that programmers perform better in areas they are passionate about, thus improving productivity. Benefits for Facebook include lower training costs, better bonding between employees, and a way to identify potential future leaders.

LivingSocial Creates the Plan Before Day 1

LivingSocial has emerged as direct competition for Groupon with its daily deals on restaurants, bars, comedy clubs, vacations, and more. It also is growing and trying to attract and retain software engineers and programmers.

The organization is really focused on the prestart phase of onboarding so that its new hires don't accept a different offer after they have accepted the one from LivingSocial.

In the acceptance conversation with the new hire, the HR partner will start to discuss what that person's 30-, 60-, and 90-day plan will look like and get her or his input. The idea is to show the new hire how "cool" the job is so that she or he won't want to talk to another company or accept another offer. LivingSocial focuses on talking about the impact of the new hire's job—emphasizing the passion of the founder, the size of the market that the company is in, and the contribution that the employee is going to make.

The Nooglers

New employees at Google are called "Nooglers" and are actually given a propeller beanie hat to wear on their first Friday. What Google does right with its new hires is to start to immerse them in the company's culture from Day 1. The company is known for its exceptional perks (free meals is the best known); however, a great deal is also expected of employees, and many Nooglers share that they started their first days and weeks on the job attending back-to-back training classes, seminars, and team meetings. They were asked to read huge amounts of documentation and start to contribute rather quickly. Much like Facebook, Google subscribes to the philosophy that people perform better in work that they are most interested in. So,

Google employees have control of 20 percent of their total project work, and this has proved highly successful for both business results and employee engagement.

Twitter Says Yes to the Desk

Twitter has made its mark in the social media market and continues to do so. Like LivingSocial, Twitter is really focused on the prestart period, from the time that the offer is accepted to Day 1. Twitter calls this process "Yes to Desk," and it's a highly coordinated effort among Recruiting, IT, and Facilities. The company knows that getting some of the logical items done and done right will make a lasting impression. As a Twitter new hire, you will get colorful PDFs sent to you to let you know what to expect on your first day. You will get the e-mail address that you want, and a T-shirt and a bottle of wine will be on your desk when you arrive on Day 1. Your desk is also strategically assigned based on the project you are working on and with whom. The CEO, Dick Costolo, has breakfast with every new employee, followed by a "company ramp-up" session that briefs new employees on teams, projects, company history, internal tools, and inside jokes. They even have reserved tables in the cafeteria so that new employees can eat lunch with their teams—there's no anxiety about whom to sit with at lunch!

Allstate Puts New Grads in Good Hands

Allstate Insurance, headquartered in Northbrook, Illinois, has an active recruiting process for new MBA graduates. Much of the recruiting is initially handled via e-mail, and one HR representative is assigned to handle all the communication with the candidates. The candidates are flown to the corporate headquarters, where they meet with several senior leaders. If there is mutual interest, an offer is extended, and the offer is often made well before the student graduates. Allstate has a 27-month rotation program (three different jobs for nine months each) for these new hires, which allows the organization to decide the best fit for these employees and also allows the employees to be able to decide which part of the organization is best for them. The new hires are assigned their first rotation placement about two months prior to Day 1. Upon their arrival, the new employees are in their respective departments with two senior managers who are responsible for overseeing the three-week onboarding program. With a department-specific focus, the onboarding experience provides information and training on the organization, its culture, and some technical skills that are required by the job. The somewhat relaxed schedule allows all the new grads to learn the organization, key business knowledge, departmental operations, and specific roles. They also benefit from formal feedback from the senior leaders who volunteered to mentor them during their transition. Allstate also allows time for and encourages the new grads to review topics on which they need extra support and allows them to network with other employees from various other departments to begin to build relationships for the future.

Gaming with Sun Microsystems

Sun Microsystems has created a unique way to engage its new hires and get them up to speed quickly. Since it hires primarily new college graduates and younger professionals, the company knew that it had to create an onboarding experience that was current and engaging. It also knew that technology would play a central role in this program. So, the Learning Services design and development group, together with the education leader, designed and built and a video game that facilitated the onboarding process. This game is interactive and fun. It allows the new employees to learn at their own pace and keeps them on track with checkpoints and reminders for due dates. It leverages the fact that most of these new employees have grown up playing video games and are comfortable with and interested in this type of learning platform.

Hospitality 101:
The Ritz-Carlton Hotel Company

The Ritz-Carlton's onboarding experience is all about the company's culture of outstanding customer service. Throughout the recruitment process, the job offer, and the orientation, the new employees are treated as well as, or even better than, the guests of this famous hotel. They enjoy a group onboarding experience, during which they hear from many of the company's top executives, learn more about the organization and its philosophies from a world-class training program, and are told that they are among the elite to have been selected as Ritz-Carlton employees. No matter what the particular role, each employee is shown how his or her contribution to the experience of the firm's clients is critical to the company's success and legacy of service.

Virtual Onboarding at IBM

This technology giant, which has reinvented itself over the last several years, has solved the challenge of onboarding a global workforce. Because IBM has thousands of employees dispersed worldwide, it had to create a consistent, scalable solution for onboarding its new hires. It has built a solution using a virtual world called Second Life. This started as an Internet game in which participants create an avatar or virtual representation of themselves in an online world and interact with others and their environments. IBM saw this as an opportunity to allow new hires from all parts of the global to gather, learn, and interact in this virtual world without ever getting on a plane. The company created onboarding meetings, facilitating training and question-and-answer sessions for all the participants, who got to know not only IBM but other new "IBM-ers" who were joining the company with them. This type of onboarding solution delivered information and also helped to build relationships among people who may never have been able to meet face-to-face.

Banking on Leaders at Bank of America

Bank of America has been extremely successful in its efforts to onboard its new and newly promoted leaders in the top three levels of the organization. Its leadership development team has created a structured, yet customized program that helps its new bank executives make the transition into their new roles. It has created a robust program that defines what it means to be a leader at B of A and how that definition translates into the bank's daily operations. The program focuses on helping "managers of managers" with development classes, coaching, and resources, especially during their first 90 days. It also makes use of peer coaches and provides a team integration process for each new leader. This is a powerful process that puts the questions and issues of the team front and center for the leaders and gives them a structure to address these questions and issues. The results of this process have come from the ability of the leaders to take on expanded roles successfully.

Full Immersion into Whirlpool Corporation

For the Whirlpool Corporation, an $18 billion company that employs 71,000 people in 66 countries, one of the most important features of its onboarding process is how it immerses all of its new employees, particularly its leaders, in the company vision, mission, and values. The company has a strong employment brand that is an extension of its product and customer service branding. It also has a rigorous selection process for its leaders and then views onboarding as an important investment in these new leaders. The onboarding program is an extension of this employment brand, which is introduced in its deep orientation and continues as the employees move into their work areas and new roles. The Whirlpool culture was added to the company vision in 2010, and it allows the company to use its culture to align new hires with the organization for a better fit. New leaders are also supported by a coaching model of onboarding that supports the emotional roller coaster they experience as they learn new roles and become accustomed to a new organization. They are supported by a strong commitment on the part of the hiring managers, who have bought into the idea that new hires require a chance to learn, build relationships, and start to "gain traction" in their roles by experiencing early success.

Getting into the Gap

The retail powerhouse Gap was onboarding long before the term became a popular buzzword in the human resources and business communities. Because of the fast pace and seasonal nature of retail, new employees can easily get overwhelmed and burn out quickly. This can be especially true for new leaders, who are hired for their past successes and have to "hit the ground running" in a highly competitive and not very forgiving environment. The Gap developed a process for its new and newly promoted leaders that allowed them the time to "learn and do." It emphasizes the importance of having clearly identified onboarding objectives, and the importance of building relationships across functions. This onboarding process encourages the new leaders to learn from their managers, peers, and team while using and sharing their own technical knowledge. It supports and promotes the building of those key relationships that are critical to projects and initiatives.

TIPS AND TAKEAWAYS FROM THIS CHAPTER

- Do your homework.

- Match updates and improvements with your objectives.

- Know what's current and what your competitors are doing.

- Always represent your brand and your culture.

CHAPTER 10

Case Study: Corporate Office Relocation as a Talent Management Strategy

Volkswagen Group of America Moves Its Headquarters to Shake Up the Talent Pool

D ave Bruce, general manager, human resources, Volkswagen Group of America (VWGoA), shared his experiences with using a corporate home office move as a talent management strategy. Dave, in addition to his day job as an HR business partner, was the project leader for this huge effort. He describes this initiative as "not just a change in address, but a change in attitude, a change in culture, and a change in our thinking as an organization." Looking at this experience in the rearview mirror, Dave reflects that overall, the company succeeded in achieving its objectives with this strategy. He emphasized that all along, the issues that the organization was struggling with in 2006 and 2007 included how it was going to be able to upgrade its workforce.

Getting Away from Dodge

Because VWGoA was located near Detroit, Michigan, it was basically "fourth in line for everything"—including talent—behind the big three automakers. There was this community of people who knew only the automotive world, and it seemed that they moved among these different organizations. The leaders at VWGoA felt like they had a holdover workforce that was getting ready to retire, was mostly resistant to change, and was a bit stale in its thinking and its ideas. Dave sums it up by describing the company's situation as being on "a downward trajectory" as it related to its talent. What the leaders were looking for was a way to reenergize their brands in the United States, especially the VW brand. Although Audi was still moving in a good direction, it had the same needs for improving its talent. In order to be more effective in highlighting the benefits of the brand to the outside world, VWGoA started to look inside its organization to make changes that would begin this transformation. The leaders knew that they needed to infuse their organization with the right people, specifically leaders that would be able to accomplish this major transformation.

Swimming with the Sharks

The choice for a home office location was not based on typical criteria like access to transportation, communication infrastructure, or tax breaks. The main objective was to select a location that would be a desirable place to live. There was little or no consideration of following other brands like Mercedes-Benz or BMW to New Jersey; instead, VW wanted to find a city where it could create its own automotive center. The president at the time had a favorite saying, "Do you want to swim with the sharks?" and the head of HR would reply, "We are going to drain that shark tank and create our own." These two leaders were adamant that they were going to "drain" the top talent from their competitors by relocating to such a desirable place that the talent would follow them there. The leadership team had the support, of course, of its German partners, who saw possibilities in expanding U.S. manufacturing in a southern state with lower labor costs. They dubbed it a "full sales offensive" to expand the brand in the United States.

Their strategy started to pay off almost immediately. As they started to talk about the move to Washington, DC, candidates who had turned them down before were now interested because of the location. Detroit was a deterrent, but now, suddenly, their new home city was a draw. The other thing that VWGoA quickly discovered, according to Dave, was that it was also attracting applicants from various other industries and experiences. There were people applying for jobs from places like AOL, American Eagle, Booz Allen, and Freddie Mac. These people were bringing fresh ideas and a new perspective, and VW was keenly aware that this would be a part of the firm's competitive edge. Also, the company was potentially creating future customers for its brands by educating them through the recruiting process about its products, its services, and who it was as a company.

The Wow! Factor

The most powerful tool in VWGoA's talent selection tool kit was undoubtedly the new building itself. The new construction and modern décor really told the story that VW and Audi were brands for the future. The lobby has a large open atrium with the latest models of both brands lined up inside. Current advertising campaigns run on large video screens, and all the public areas are sleek yet welcoming. A café and a fitness center are prominent features of the first floor, and open, modern office space with glass walls for the executives populates the upper floors. "The building told our success story," Bruce explains as he also says that for him, this experience was a "career-defining" one, because, he went on, "You get to create a whole new company."

Lessons Learned

Overall, VWGoA's move to Washington, DC, was a successful one, and the company accomplished its objectives of upgrading its talent and growing its brands. This move was not without its challenges, however. One of the most obvious bumps in the road was a bit of a culture clash.

Some conflict occurred between the employees who had relocated from Michigan and the ones who were hired locally. Bruce describes many of the differences as being between the more traditional midwestern work ethic and the value placed on tenure; and the mid-Atlantic (DC) style, which is more tech-savvy, more laid back, and more mobile (many people had had three jobs in three years, and this was not considered unusual). The HR team had to adjust and align the thinking of these two distinct groups and help leaders understand that the diversity in thinking and styles would ultimately be one of the company's strengths, not a barrier.

The culture has successfully morphed into one that uses the more tech-savvy and progressive mid-Atlantic view of the world to leverage the midwestern work ethic. There are still opportunities to improve, but Dave calls it a successful implementation that positions VWGoA for long-term growth in the United States. The organization has become a "destination" for employees and not just a step along the way.

TIPS AND TAKEAWAYS FROM THIS CHAPTER

- Consider headquarters relocations as a talent management strategy.

- Drain that shark tank and create your own!

- Develop a competitive edge by attracting workers from different industries and experience—not all talent need come from your business arena.

- Tell people you are a brand for the future. Up your "Wow" factor!

Conclusion

Whether you are considering a corporate relocation, overhauling your HR business partner alignment, or simply tweaking your employment brand as a way to renew your talent strategy, the important thing is that you continuously look to update and refresh the way you select and bring onboard your new talent. Given the constant changes in technology and the evolving demographics of our workforce, the organizations that embrace and leverage these changes will enjoy a competitive advantage in the ongoing war for talent.

It's Not All About the Money

The good news, as we have found through our work and research, is that the companies that are most successful in recruiting and retaining the best talent are not necessarily those that spend the most money. Representing your organization authentically, having a strong point of view as an employer, and communicating that point of view openly and honestly to your potential candidates and new hires are the keys to successful recruitment. These elements are not expensive, but they do require you to take the time to develop them, and they also need the buy-in and alignment of the whole organization. Candidates are savvy and can tell when employment brands are artificial or when there is a "sales version" of the organization's culture that is shown during recruitment, with the real culture being revealed after the offer has been extended or during a weak onboarding experience.

Six Simple Steps

In our work with clients, we have developed six simple steps for creating an effective talent selection and onboarding experience for your organization. *Simple* is a relative term here because, while the steps are simple to explain and understand, their execution can be more difficult depending on where you are as an organization.

Step 1: Define Your Objectives

No initiative has a solid foundation or is sustainable without clear and defined objectives. You would be amazed at how many companies jump right into designing a program or solution without taking the time to align the organization and the project team around the desired objectives. Without these objectives as a touchstone, the initiatives often get off track and do not have metrics to support them.

For example, the objective might be to improve the quality of our incoming talent to support our growth goal of 20 percent by 2020.

Step 2: Identify Your Audiences

After you have your objectives clearly defined, the next step is to identify the audiences that you most want to affect and influence with your talent strategy. There are several options, and again, by taking the time to articulate each one and gain alignment within the organization, you reduce the risk of making the wrong assumptions and missing the mark on your objectives.

For example, your sample audiences might be new leaders, people with high potential, external hires, internal promotions, cross-functional transfers, new graduates, experienced hires, contract workers, and the like.

Step 3: Create Roles and Responsibilities

For some organizations, once they have completed the first two steps in this process, there is a temptation to start creating the solution. However, without Steps 3 and 4, your organization will probably spend more time in rework and cleanup after implementing a half-baked program than it would have spent planning these steps. Creating clear roles and responsibilities for all partners in your new program is the "secret sauce" for an effective strategy. By talking through each person's role at a high level, you can create a "filter" for every future decision about who does what in your process. This is extremely helpful in facilitating any kind of update or change because assumptions are made based on how things used to be or should be.

For example, recruiters are responsible for all interactions with the new hires from initial contact to job offer and will work with the HR partner to provide a "warm handoff" upon acceptance.

Step 4: Capture Your Culture

Knowing and being able to articulate your organization's actual culture, not the aspirational one, will serve you well as you work to update and improve your talent strategy. By bringing the dos and don'ts in the organization to the surface and then incorporating those data into your programs, you will give your new hires the best chance of being successful because they can map their behaviors onto the desired behaviors in your culture. Many skilled and competent employees have failed to integrate successfully and then end up leaving either voluntarily or involuntarily, resulting in a loss for both the employee and the employer. Bringing to the surface, documenting, and then communicating your cultural data is a critical component of your talent strategy.

Step 5: Build the Solution

Using the foundational work that you have done in the first four steps, you can now create the process pieces for your talent selection and onboarding programs. One thing to consider is taking inventory of what is working well now so that you can keep it. Do you have a killer orientation or pre-start package? Incorporate what you are doing well into your updated strategy so that you can continue to build on your success. Another tip is to research best practices in your industry and even outside it for some great examples.

Step 6: Measure the Impact

Creating metrics that measure the success of your overall objectives is the last step in this process. With the right metrics, you will be able to continue to support the business case for your talent strategy and demonstrate its value to the organization. The focus on measurement will only continue to increase and be important. Continue to track the data that are meaningful and add data that match your updated objectives. Ways to collect this information include time-based surveys of your new hires and hiring managers, feedback from your candidate pools, success rates of assessments, and qualitative data collected throughout the recruitment and onboarding processes. Data on the engagement of new hires and their speed to productivity are also good indicators of the impact of your talent strategy.

Meeting the changing demands of organizations is tough, but HR professionals and line leaders can adapt their talent acquisition and onboarding strategies to support their complex business goals. Evaluating which talent tools to keep and which to switch out is a great place to start. By staying focused on the overall objectives, putting in the time to define those objectives, and getting buy-in and alignment from the key partners, your organization will realize the benefits of an updated and improved strategy.

Jim Collins said it best:
"Great vision without great people is irrelevant."

Appendix

The talent selection and onboarding process is the first important step in a new associate's development and success. Whether you are making such a transition yourself or coaching someone else through it, our best advice is that you to create a strategy and stick to it.

Here are several additional resources for you to use in your talent selection and onboarding processes. These will provide extra guidance for you or your new talent as they come onboard.

For best results, re-create these resources with your employment brand and make them your own.

Congratulations! You're making a difference!

	New Leader 30–60–90-Day Onboarding Plan						
√	Onboarding Action Item	Prestart	Week 1	30 Days	60 Days	90 Days	Resources
	Getting Prepared • Read and review company briefing information	▬					Briefing portfolio Company website

	Getting Started
	Complete:
	  • Office logistics
	  • New hire orientation
	  • Personal and/or relocation items
			▬				Logistics checklist
							
							Smart starts

	Core Company Onboarding Objectives • Understand strategic vision • Understand overall organization • Understand competitive landscape • Understand company financials • Understand company culture • Understand decision-making process			▬ ▬			
	Onboarding Meeting I Meet with hiring manager to identify key onboarding objectives and early wins		▬				Meeting agenda(s)

New Leader 30–60–90-Day Onboarding Plan *(continued)*							
√	Onboarding Action Item	Prestart	Week 1	30 Days	60 Days	90 Days	Resources
	Individual Onboarding Objectives • Clarify role and expectations • Manage personal and family transitions • Start community network		▬▬▬▬▬▬▬▬▬▬				Role clarity tool
	Stakeholder Analysis • Begin to identify key stakeholders and set up meet and greet schedule		▬▬▬▬▬▬				List of people who support these objectives
	Getting the Culture • Observe and begin to understand behaviors, norms, and work environment		▬▬▬▬▬▬				Suggested questions to surface the culture
	Core Business Unit (BU) Onboarding Objectives • Understand BU structure • Understand BU strategy • Understand financials • Understand BU's role in the overall organization • Understand the culture in the BU		▬▬▬▬▬▬▬▬				Links Reports Presentations that support each objective

	New Leader 30–60–90-Day Onboarding Plan *(continued)*						
√	Onboarding Action Item	Prestart	Week 1	30 Days	60 Days	90 Days	Resources
	Onboarding Meeting II Meet with hiring manager and HR support to gain feedback: • Against objectives • Against culture				▬		Meeting agenda(s)
	Team alignment process				▬		Process overview
	Personal Transition: • How am I feeling about the transition? • Have I made community and personal connections? • Have my family and/ or my significant other made the transition appropriately?				▬		
	Performance Management: • Do I understand the transition to the company's performance management process?					▬	Performance management process

Smart Starts for New Hires

Purpose

To give new hires tips on the types of behaviors that will help them be successful in the company's culture.

How to Use

The new hire should refer to the tips given here while implementing his or her onboarding plan. The tips will give him or her direction as to how to be successful as he or she integrates into the new role and culture.

- Identify others, both within and outside of the organization, with whom you need to build relationships.

- Make sure that you are clear about your role and performance expectations for your first 30, 60, and 90 days.

- Manage expectations; deliver on commitments.

- Expect surprises concerning your role, your partners, and the organization. Use your onboarding process and resources to manage the surprises.

- Ask lots of questions and actively listen as you learn.

- Make sure that you understand the history and ownership of anything that you want to change.

- Understand the organization's politics.

- Early on, avoid high-risk initiatives; secure early wins to establish credibility.

- Manage your time. Prioritize and be structured, allowing flexibility for unexpected demands.

- Give priority to your hiring manager's priorities.

Role Clarity Discussion Tool

Purpose

To provide an outline for a discussion with a new associate and his or her manager to talk about the role, what the specific expectations for it are, and how it fits in with the larger team and organization.

1. Talking points:

   - Outline your understanding of your role and the key deliverables.

- Compare your understanding with the actual tasks and assignments your manager (or others) has given you. Is there a disconnect, and if so, what is it?

- Talk about gaps, prioritize tasks, and develop an action plan on how to address the disconnects.

2. Tips on Talking with Your Manager:

- Assess your manager's style—how does he or she prefer to communicate; what are his or her areas of focus and hot buttons; does he or she focus on the details or the big picture?

- Plan your conversation based on your manager's style: how he or she can best receive the information and how it will help your manager meet his or her goals.

- Determine whether it is best to add this conversation to another meeting or to set up a separate meeting. Is it best to have the meeting at the office or over lunch or coffee outside of the office?

- Ask to schedule a follow-up meeting to make sure the action plan will stick.

Early Wins Worksheet

Purpose

To help you as a new leader plan "early win" deliverables, understand their importance to the organization, and identify the resources needed for success in delivering the early win; and also identify the six initiatives or work products that could be used to gauge your effectiveness as a new leader over the first three or four months in your position. Review your plan with your human resources partner and your hiring manager to align expectations and determine the appropriate resources.

Deliverable and Timing (and Related Expectations)	How It Supports Larger (or Longer-Term) New Leader Performance Objective	Resources Required

Deliverable and Timing (and Related Expectations)	How It Supports Larger (or Longer-Term) New Leader Performance Objective	Resources Required

Feedback Impact Curve

This feedback impact curve illustrates the impact of early feedback for a new hire—with it, he or she is more likely to succeed; without it, success comes hard or not at all. Stakeholders' perceptions are formed early, and without adjustments in a new hire's behaviors, they may never improve.

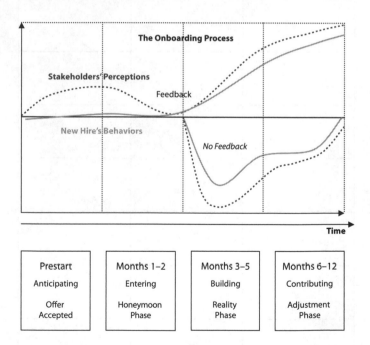

It is important for new hires, especially leaders, to get actionable feedback in their first 45 to 60 days on the job so that they can make appropriate changes. Using a survey tool that is specifically aimed at collecting onboarding feedback—not performance feedback—is critical.

Notes

Introduction

1. Jennifer Alsever, "Objective: Hire Top Talent," 100 Best Companies to Work For, *Fortune* magazine, February 2014.
2. Lydia Abbot, "How to Kickstart Your Mobile Recruiting Program/Talent Blog," November 19, 2013, http://talent.linkedin.com/blog/index.php/2013/11/how-to-kickstart-your-mobile-recruiting-program.

Chapter 1

1. U.S. Bureau of Labor Statistics, "Spotlight on Statistics: The Recession of 2007–2009," February 2013, p. 2, http://www.bls.gov/spotlight/2012/recession/pdf/recession_bls_spotlight.pdf.
2. Ibid., p. 7.
3. Robert Kurzban and Jason Weeden, "HurryDate: Mate Preferences in Action," *Evolution and Human Behavior* 26 (2005), pp. 227–244.

Chapter 2

1. David Ulrich, *Human Resource Champions* (Boston: Harvard Business School Press, 1996). p. 7.

Chapter 4

1. Victor Luckerson, "The 10 Absolute Worst Buzzwords to Put on a Resume," *Time*, December 11, 2013, TIME.com http://business.time.com/2013/12/11/the-10-absolute-worst-buzzwords-to-put-on-a-resume/#ixzz2rkRjutXJ.

Chapter 6

1. Brenda Hampel and Erika Lamont, *Perfect Phrases for New Employee Orientation and Onboarding* (New York: McGraw-Hill, 2011).

Index

About the Authors

Erika Lamont has worked with hundreds of operational leaders in order to support them in selecting, assessing, and developing their talent and their business processes. She has worked with clients to create customized solutions for their business challenges, which include leadership coaching, leading others through change, onboarding, and team dynamics.

She, along with Brenda Hampel, is a founding partner of Connect the Dots Consulting and has worked with clients that include Audi of America, the Ohio State University, Volkswagen Group of America, Cardinal Health, Tween Brands, Lane Bryant, Nissan USA, and the Wexner Medical Center at Ohio State University.

Erika has also held leadership roles in supply chain management at Riverside Methodist Hospital, part of the OhioHealth Corporation, and Bath & Body Works. She brings a distinctive blend of operational experience and leadership development skills to her client base.

Erika has coauthored two other books, *Solving Employee Performance Problems: How to Spot Problems Early, Take Appropriate Action, and Bring Out the Best in Everybody* (McGraw-Hill) and *Perfect Phrases for New Employee Orientation and Onboarding* (McGraw-Hill).

When she is not working or writing, Erika enjoys cooking, trying new restaurants, and hanging out with her family: her husband, Michael, and her daughters, Elizabeth and Maggie.

For more information about solving your talent challenges, contact Erika at 614-793-8835, elamont@connectthe dotsconsulting.com, and visit our website at www.connect thedotsconsulting.com.

Anne Bruce knows how to engage, evaluate, attract, nurture, and develop top talent! Her popular keynote speech and seminar workshop, "America's Got Talent in the Workplace and It Comes from All Over the World," has received rave reviews from Dallas to Dubai. Anne is a bestselling author with 20 books published to date, including *Discover True North: A Four-Week Approach to Ignite Your Passion and Activate Your Potential* (McGraw-Hill), *Be Your Own Mentor* (McGraw-Hill), *The Manager's Guide to Motivating Employees* (McGraw-Hill), *Solving Employee Performance Problems* (McGraw-Hill), *Perfect Phrases for Documenting Employee*

Performance Problems, Perfect Phrases for Employee Development Plans (McGraw-Hill), *Mighty Manager Series: How to Motivate Every Employee* (McGraw-Hill), *Leaders Start to Finish: A Roadmap for Developing Top Performers,* 2d ed. (ASTD Press), and *Speak for a Living: The Insider's Guide to Building a Speaking Career* (ASTD Press).

Anne has had the privilege of speaking, writing, or training at prestigious venues and for organizations, such as the White House, the Pentagon, Saks Fifth Avenue, Sony International, GEICO, Southwest Airlines, JetBlue, Ben & Jerry's, Baylor University Medical Center, MedAmerica Billing Services, Inc. (MBSI), Harvard and Stanford law schools, and the Conference Board of Europe.

For details on how to bring this book's training program to your organization, and for information on additional motivational leadership programs like "The Art of Leadership," "Communications Excellence," "Going from Customer Service Excellence to Customer Service Loyalty," "Performance Coaching for Success," and "Nurturing the Technical Professional," contact Anne by calling her at **214-507-8242** or e-mailing her at **Anne@Anne Bruce.com**. Please visit her on LinkedIn and on her "Fans of Anne Bruce" page on Facebook or check out her website at www.AnneBruce.com for more information, scheduling press interviews, availability and fees.

AVAILABLE IN PRINT AND EBOOK

Quick-Access HR Toolkits
from Training Experts Anne Bruce,
Erika Lamont and Brenda Hampel!

Leverage top talent to drive
organizational success